The Commandments

Chris A. Legebow

ISBN-13: 978-1-988914-03-9

DEDICATION

I thank God for the excellent foundation teaching I received in the churches I have been a part of.

Chris A. Legebow

CONTENTS

ACKNOWLEDGMENTS

All scripture taken from Bible Gateway.com
Modern English Version (MEV)
.

1 INTRODUCTION

The Commandments of God

Because the commandments are no longer taught in our public schools, many people do not know the commandments given to Moses by God on Mount Sinai. God literally wrote the commandments on the side of the mountain and carved 2 tablets of stone and gave them to Moses so he could teach them to Israel. They are the basis for many of our existing laws and government in North America.

If you do not know the commandments or have not received teaching on them, it is my hope that you will learn them. If you are not a Christian, it is my prayer you will receive Jesus the Messiah who fulfilled not only these commandments but who lived holy and died for our sins.

If you are a Christian but desire to know more about the commandments, it is my prayer you will prayerfully consider each of the commandments. My writing about them is to show a Biblical scriptural interpretation of them. If God should convict you while your reading, please, repent, accept Jesus Christ's blood shed for you that you might be cleansed. Jesus Christ paid the penalty of our sins. Not only will you be forgiven, but you can be set free so you no longer sin. God never condemns you. If you feel condemnation, plead the blood of Jesus over yourself because it is an evil spirit attacking you. God brings conviction in His mercy so you can be forgiven and cleansed.

1 John 1: 9 If we confess our sins, He is faithful and just to forgive us our sins and cleanse us from all unrighteousness. 10

It is my hope that you will not only learn the commandments but teach them to your family members. They were considered so important that Moses was commanded by God to give them and teach them to Israel and they were instructed to teach them to their children throughout generations. The Word of God is important because they help us align our lives properly with God's Word and his will. Only by the Holy Spirit living inside of us can be keep the commandments and live holy.

2 CHAPTER

The commandments
1st commandment

Moses

God used Moses to deliver Israel out of Egyptian bondage after 400 years of slavery. God showed mighty signs and miracles, finally with the death of the first born including Pharaoh's son, Pharaoh's heart was softened to let Israel go free from captivity. Moses lead them to the Red Sea, God parted the Red Sea as Moses raised his staff over it. Moses lead the people to Mount Sinai where Moses received instruction from God. God wrote with his finger onto the side of Mount Sinai and carved two stone tablets out of the rock. God desired to restore fellowship with Israel and promised to give them the land of Abraham's promise. The people who served God in Egypt did not know God except through oral storytelling. They believed and hoped for a deliverer to arise to set them free from captivity.

God knew that Israel did not know His ways or His paths. God gave the commandments so that people would know how to live pleasing to God so their ways would be blessed and they would have abundance, prosperity and peace. Those who gathered at Mount Sinai were given freedom. They were given rules by which their lives would have God's blessing.

God had given Moses the core of all the laws and commandments on those tablets. There are a total of 613 Levitical laws and commandments. The core of them are in the ten commandments.

God promised to bless those who would keep his laws. To 'be Blessed' means total blessing or total prosperity in every area of life: health, relationships, career, work, leisure, creativity etc. It is God's delight to bless those who honour Him and are in covenant with Him. Covenant is that those who would obey these commandments, God Himself would bless them and cause them to multiply in number and strength. If the idea of being blessed or receiving the blessing is unfamiliar to you, please research some of these teachers as they preach the word of God with faith in the blessing: Kenneth and Gloria Copeland, Creflo Dollar, Jesse Duplantis, Jerry Savelle, Bill Winston, Benny Hinn, Marilyn Hickey, Joel Osteen etc. There are many preachers who literally believe that God delights in giving us His best as we live in communion with Him.

My book will study the commandments in depth. Once, every child in Canada or the United States learned these commandments in the school system. At present, children would only learn these commandments by their parents teaching them or from church. God instructed Moses to teach them, to keep them and to have the people know the commandments. The commandments cover all aspects of human life. They can be summarized as two main parts: the commandments related to God, and the commandments related to man.

List of Commandments

Deuteronomy 5: 6 I am the Lord, your God, who brought you out of the land of Egypt, from the house of bondage.

7 You shall have no other gods before Me.

8 You shall not make yourself any graven image, or any likeness of anything that is in heaven above, or that is in the earth beneath, or that is in the waters beneath the earth; 9 you shall not bow down to them, nor serve them. For I, the Lord your God, am a jealous God, visiting the iniquity of the fathers on the children, and on the third and fourth generations of those who hate Me, 10 but showing mercy to thousands of them that love Me and keep My commandments.

11 You shall not take the name of the Lord your God in vain, for the Lord will not exonerate anyone who takes His name in vain.

12 Keep the Sabbath day, to keep it holy, just as the Lord your God has commanded you. 13 Six days you shall labor and do all your work, 14 but the seventh day is the Sabbath of the Lord your God. On it you shall not do any work: you, nor your son, nor your daughter, nor your male servant, nor your female servant, nor your ox, nor your donkey, nor any of your livestock, nor the foreigner that is within your gates, so that your male servant and your female servant may rest as well as you. 15 Remember that you were a servant in the land of Egypt, and that the Lord your God brought you out from there with a mighty hand and by an outstretched arm; therefore your God commanded you to keep the Sabbath day.

16 Honor your father and your mother, just as the Lord your God has commanded you, that your days may be prolonged, and that it may go well with you in the land which the Lord your God is giving you.

17 You shall not murder.

18 You shall not commit adultery.

19 You shall not steal.

20 You shall not bear false witness against your neighbor.

21 You shall not covet your neighbor's wife, nor shall you covet your neighbor's house, his field, his male servant, his female servant, his ox, his donkey, or anything that belongs to your neighbor.

1st Commandment

In the first commandment, God is reminding Israel that God is the one who delivered them out of Egyptian bondage. God is ONE. There are no other gods. God makes it clear that there can be no other gods worshipped.

In some countries, Christians may preach about God and the people will gladly receive God as one of their gods. They will worship other gods also. God commandments that there can be no other god worshipped. He demands full allegiance. He expects total acknowledgement that He alone is God. He revealed Himself to Moses as "IAM that I AM" (Exodus 3: 14) The tetragrammaton JHVH – we translate it into the word Jehovah.

Deuteronomy 5: 6 I am the Lord, your God, who brought you out of the land of Egypt, from the house of bondage.

7 You shall have no other gods before Me.

King Solomon was given an awesome privilege to build a Temple for the LORD. King David had saved gold and silver and trees and precious stones etc. all his life because it was his desire to build God a temple, but God said that Solomon would do it. David obeyed God. His heart was passionate about God so he gathered all the precious aspects for building and had the plans for the temple etc. ready so that Solomon would only have to oversee the construction.

2 Chronicles 7 explains that upon the building of the Temple, and the sacrifices offered to God, the glory of God filled the temple. The presence of God was so strong that the priests were not able to minister anymore because the glory of God's presence was so thick. I believe they experienced being slain in the Spirit but didn't know the term of it.

Solomon prays a strong dedicatory prayer over the Temple. It shows his total obedience to King David. He did what he was told he must do. He knew God had chosen him to do it. I'm not sure if there is anything more satisfying than doing what you know you were created to do. His prayer over the temple is that God's holy presence in the ark of the covenant will always remain in the midst of his people. His prayer is that even if the people turn away from God, but later repent and pray, God will forgive them. He prays consecrating the structure to God's glory so that if people should even turn their face towards the place, God will hear their prayers and forgive them. All of these verses, plus Solomon's lavish sacrifices to God were a sign of God's blessing on Solomon and on King David because God had promised King David that God would raise up a people who would be mighty and eventually the birth of the Messiah would come from his lineage.

As you read the scriptures, see how the heart of Solomon was wholly turned to God. His prayer is for the people of Israel all who will be born of Israel. Solomon has a view of the future promised to Abraham – a seed as vast as the stars of the sky or as grains of sand on a beach. Solomon was wholly serving Jehovah. The commandments given to Moses were in the Ark of the covenant in the most Holy place – the Holy of Holies. Although thousands of years had passed, God kept his promise to Abraham. God kept His promise to Moses. Israel was abiding in the promised land. Finally, a place of worship was built for the Ark of the covenant. All the laws of Moses would be taught in that temple. All the commandments would be taught. People would enter the outer court and pray – even Gentiles could pray there. In the Holy place, an inner chamber, there were priests ministering to God with worship and with the lighting of candles and incense. They remembered God's gift of manna that had fed them for 40 years in the wilderness. There was a table that had showbread on it. The Temple was a special fulfillment of prophesies for thousands of years. God's glory showed His pleasure at this culmination of worship.

Prayer over the Temple as a dedicated Holy Place

2 Chronicles 6: 18 "For will God indeed dwell with man on the earth? The heavens, even the highest heavens, are not able to contain You, much less

this house that I have built. 19 But respond to the prayer of Your servant and to his plea, O Lord my God, to listen to the cry and prayer of Your servant who prays before You, 20 that Your eyes might be open toward this house both day and night, to the place that You have said that You will set Your name, in order to hear the prayer of Your servant for this place. 21 And listen to the pleas of Your servant and Your people Israel when they pray toward this place. And may You respond from heaven, the place of Your dwelling, so that You hear and forgive.

Prayer for those who have sinned to find repentance

22 "If a man sins against his companion, and the companion swears and puts him under a curse, and the wronged man comes with an oath before Your altar at this temple, 23 then You will hear from heaven, and You will act and judge Your servants, to repay the guilty one by bringing his way on his own head; and to vindicate the innocent one by rendering to him according to his righteous behavior.

Prayer for those who are fighting or in need of God's help

24 "If Your people Israel are struck before enemies because they have sinned against You, and they return and confess Your name and pray and seek Your favor in this house, 25 then You will hear from heaven and forgive the sin of Your people Israel, and You will bring them back to the land that You gave them and their fathers.

Prayer if the people had sinned so there was no rain

26 "When the sky is shut up and there is no rain because they have sinned against You, and they pray toward this place and confess Your name and turn from their sin when You afflict them, 27 then You will hear from heaven and forgive the sin of Your servants and Your people Israel because You will teach them the good path in which they will walk, and You will send rain on the land that You have given to Your people as a possession.

Prayer if the people had sinned and the land was cursed as with the curse of Adam

28 "When there is famine in the land or when there is pestilence, blight, mildew, winged locust, or grasshopper, or when enemies besiege them in the land up to their city gates, in whatever plague or sickness, 29 whatever prayer or plea that is made by any man or by all your people Israel, when each man knows his own affliction and his own sorrow, and stretches out

his hands toward this house, 30 then You will hear from heaven, the place of the habitation of Your dwelling, and forgive, and You will render to each according to his conduct, for You know their hearts (for You alone know the heart of people), 31 so that they may fear You and walk in Your ways all the days that they live on the land that You have given to our fathers.

Prayer so that strangers could come to know the one true God

32 "When foreigners are not from Your people Israel and come from a distant land, because of Your great name, mighty hand, and outstretched arm, and they come and pray toward this house, 33 then hear from heaven, from Your dwelling place, and act on everything for which the foreigner calls on You, that all the peoples of the earth may know Your name and fear You, as do Your people Israel; and that they may know that this house which I have built is called by Your name.

Prayer for those in battles

34 "When Your people go out to battle against their enemies, in the way that You send them, and when they pray to You toward this city that You have chosen and the house that I have built for Your name, 35 then hear from heaven their prayer and plea and act for their cause.

Prayer for those who earnestly seek God with all their hearts

36 "When they sin against You (for there is no one who does not sin) and You are angry against them and give them to their enemies, and they are taken captive to a land, whether distant or near, 37 and they turn their hearts in the land that they have been taken captive, and they repent and seek Your favor in the land of captivity saying, 'We have sinned, done wrong, and acted wickedly,' 38 and if they turn in repentance to You with all their heart and all their soul in the land of their captivity that they were taken to, and pray toward the land that You have given to their fathers, and toward the city that You have chosen, and toward the house that I have built for Your name, 39 then hear from heaven, from Your dwelling place, their prayer and supplication, and maintain their cause, and forgive the people who have sinned against You.

Prayer of conclusion of dedication

40 "Now, O my God, may Your eyes be open and Your ears attentive to the prayer that I offer in this place.

41 "Now rise up, O Lord God, to Your resting place,
both You and the ark of Your strength.
And let Your priests, O Lord God, be clothed in salvation
and Your loyal ones rejoice in goodness.
42 O Lord God, do not turn Your face from Your anointed.
Remember the mercies of Your servant David."

Because of God's pleasure, He appears to Solomon in a dream and instructs him. He speaks the terms of His covenant with Israel. He promises to be merciful, to forgive those who truly repent. He promises to bring restoration of relationship with the people who repent and also the blessing. The blessing covers the earth and the conditions of life on earth as well as person peace with God.

God accepts the Temple as a place for His Holy presence.

I have heard your prayer, and I have chosen for Myself in this place a house of sacrifice.

13 "When I shut up the heaven and there is no rain, or when I command
the locusts to devour the land, or send pestilence on My people, 14 if My
people, who are called by My name, will humble themselves and pray, and
seek My face and turn from their wicked ways, then I will hear from
heaven, and will forgive their sin and will heal their land. 15 Now My eyes
will be open and My ears attentive to the prayer of this place. 16 So now I
have chosen and consecrated this house that My name be there continually.
My eyes and heart will be there for all days.

God makes a special pledge to Solomon but it is conditional. He says that Solomon must obey the ways of God and the words of God as David lived with passion for God so must Solomon. He says if Solomon will live wholly unto God, God will bless him and his lineage – the condition is that Solomon must wholly follow the LORD.

17 "And you, if you walk before Me as David your father did to do
everything that I command you to do, and you keep My statutes and
judgments, 18 then I will set the throne of your kingdom as I made a
covenant with David your father saying, 'You will not lack a man to rule
Israel.'

God gives the condition for the blessing on the people of Israel. It is also conditional. If the people will live according to God's commandments, they will know blessing and God's presence will be in their midst. If they disobey God and turn away from Him, to worship other gods, God will abandon them and they will live in conditions of the curse of Adam.

19 "But if the people turn aside and abandon My statutes and commandments that I have given to you, and you walk after and serve other gods and worship them, 20 then I will uproot them from My land that I have given to them; and the house that I have consecrated for My name, I will throw it from before Me and set it as a proverb and taunt among the peoples. 21 And even though this house was majestic, it will lie desolate before all who pass by it, and they will say, 'Why did the Lord do such a thing to this land and this house?' 22 Then they will say, 'Because they abandoned the Lord, the God of their fathers who brought them up from the land of Egypt, and they took hold of other gods and worshipped and served them; therefore He has brought on them all this disaster."

That day of the dedication of the Temple of God and Solomon's heart in agreement with God starts what could have been a glory for all of Israel for all of Solomon's life. It was not what happened though. In chapter 2 Chronicles 8, Solomon sends for the queen of Egypt to be his wife. He chose a woman who serves the idols of Egypt. Egypt was the place of bondage and oppression. They had many pagan gods. Solomon who is the most important person in Israel sets a poor standard of marrying an unbeliever. God strictly warns against marrying unbelievers because they will sway a believer to worship other gods.

Solomon had prosperity beyond what any one can imagine. Solomon has anything He should desire. His kingdom is in peace. God's Holy presence is with them. All he must do is live a holy godly life worshipping God and caring for the people to know peace and the blessing of the LORD.

1 Kings 11 But King Solomon loved many foreign women in addition to the daughter of Pharaoh, women of the Moabites, Ammonites, Edomites, Sidonians, and Hittites, 2 from the nations which the Lord warned the children of Israel about, saying, "You shall not go in to them, nor shall they come in to you, for they will surely turn your heart away toward their gods." Solomon clung to these in love. 3 He had seven hundred wives who were princesses and three hundred concubines, and his wives turned his heart away. 4 For when Solomon was old, his wives turned his heart away after other gods, and his heart was not perfect with the Lord his God as the heart of David his father had been. 5 For Solomon went after Ashtoreth, the goddess of the Sidonians, and after Molek, the abomination of the

Ammonites. 6 Solomon did what was evil in the sight of the Lord and did not fully follow the Lord as his father David had done.

7 Then Solomon built a high place for Chemosh, the abomination of Moab, in the hill that is close to Jerusalem, and for Molek, the abomination of the children of Ammon. 8 He did the same for all his foreign wives, who burned incense and sacrificed to their gods.

The same Solomon who was raised in David's kingdom honouring God, the same Solomon who built the Temple of God, is the same Solomon who abandoned God. He lusted after beautiful women and many of them. They persuaded him to build pagan temples for other gods. What Solomon did is worse than denying God. He kept the Temple of God but also had other gods. This is a direct breaking of the first commandment of having no other gods.

Solomon's pagan shrines, turned the hearts of Israel to other gods. The very thing that God warned him of occurs. Israel no longer wholly worships God and Solomon's children were not raised as worshippers of God but of pagan gods. The Kingdom that was promised to King David, has become corrupted by Solomon who could have made a difference for all of the history of Israel – the future of Israel. There are a series of kings who come after him, some terribly wicked; some servants of God who bring a restoration of the people to God. Solomon's sins against God affected all of Israel present and future. Eventually the Temple is captured and in ruin. All the gold, silver, precious jewels are taken by pagan armies. It remains a ruin until the rebuilding of the temple because of Nehemiah and Ezra the prophets thousands of years later.

No Other gods

Having no other gods, may mean different things besides actual pagan gods. Some people love God but they love money more than God. Some people love things more than God. Whatever you live your life serving if it is not Jehovah God, is a false god. It is important that God be the only one we give our lives to. Use things; God wants to bless us with things so we have whatever we need. Use money; God wants to prosper us financially. Only love God with all your being. It is a heart decision that affects daily decisions in what we do, say and how we live our lives.

Some people falsely believe that Christians believe in 3 gods. It is not true. We believe in One God who expresses Himself in 3 distinct personalities:

Jehovah, Jesus, Holy Spirit.

Jehovah God is the God who revealed himself to Moses and the saints of the Old Testament

"I Am that I Am"

Exodus 3: 14 And God said to Moses, "I AM WHO I AM,"[a] and He said, "You will say this to the children of Israel, 'I AM has sent me to you.'

God revealed Himself to Moses and Israel with this term. The translation of it Is Jehovah..
Jesus Christ came to earth in the womb of Mary a Virgin because God promised to send a Messiah or deliverer to His people. Jesus Christ the Messiah is known as the Saviour. He died on a cross to save us from our sins and iniquities.

John 3: 16 "For God so loved the world that He gave His only begotten Son, that whoever believes in Him should not perish, but have eternal life. 17 For God did not send His Son into the world to condemn the world, but that the world through Him might be saved. 18 He who believes in Him is not condemned. But he who does not believe is condemned already, because he has not believed in the name of the only begotten Son of God.

Jesus promised to send the Holy Spirit to comfort those who believed in Him. The Holy Spirit is the presence of God who comes to live inside of the spirit of each believer in Jesus Christ.

John 20: 21 So Jesus said to them again, "Peace be with you. As My Father has sent Me, even so I send you." 22 When He had said this, He breathed on them and said to them, "Receive the Holy Spirit. 23 If you forgive the sins of anyone, they are forgiven them. If you retain the sins of anyone, they are retained."

Acts 2: 8 But you shall receive power when the Holy Spirit comes upon you. And you shall be My witnesses in Jerusalem, and in all Judea and Samaria, and to the ends of the earth."

There are 3 expressions of God but only one God. Just as water can be a liquid, it can be frozen to make a solid. It can boil and become a vapour. All three forms of water are still water. There are 3 distinct expressions of God but only one God.

3 CHAPTER

The 2nd commandment

Deuteronomy 5: 8 You shall not make yourself any graven image, or any likeness of anything that is in heaven above, or that is in the earth beneath, or that is in the waters beneath the earth; 9 you shall not bow down to them, nor serve them. For I, the Lord your God, am a jealous God, visiting the iniquity of the fathers on the children, and on the third and fourth generations of those who hate Me, 10 but showing mercy to thousands of them that love Me and keep My commandments.

In this commandment, similar to the first, the focus is on worshipping and honouring only God. In the Scriptures, Jehovah God is the only God who does not appear in the image of an idol. An idol is a statue or painting or carving or representation of a false god. In the above commandment, God strictly forbids any representation of Himself.

Adam and Eve knew God's presence although He did not appear to them. God spoke with them and talked with them each evening. They knew His presence even though no image is given. The sound of His presence is how they knew Him.

Genesis 3: 8 Then they heard the sound of the Lord God walking in the garden in the cool of the day, and the man and his wife hid themselves from the presence of the Lord God among the trees of the garden.

God speaks to Abram and even though he lived among idol worshippers in Ur of the Chaldeans, he didn't see God but knew God as the one true God by his voice. Abram was called out from his people and given a promise by God that he would be blessed.

Genesis 11: 12 Now the Lord said to Abram, "Go from your country, your family, and your father's house to the land that I will show you.

2 I will make of you a great nation;
  I will bless you
and make your name great,
  so that you will be a blessing.
3 I will bless them who bless you

and curse him who curses you,[a]
and in you all families of the earth
will be blessed."

4 So Abram departed, as the Lord had spoken to him, and Lot went with him. Abram was seventy-five years old when he departed from Harran. 5

He gives Abraham memorable encounters such as in Genesis 15 where God makes covenant with him by consuming the sacrifice Abraham makes. He uses the starry sky to show Abraham the number of descendants he will have.

Genesis 26: 4 I will make your descendants multiply as the stars of the heavens and will give your descendants all these lands. By your descendants all the nations of the earth will be blessed,[a

God appears to Jacob in a dream and reveals himself as the one true God.

Genesis 28: 10 Then Jacob went out from Beersheba and went toward Harran. 11 He came to a certain place and stayed there all night, because the sun had set. He took one of the stones of that place and put it under his head, and lay down in that place to sleep. 12 He dreamed and saw a ladder set up on the earth with the top of it reaching to heaven. The angels of God were ascending and descending on it. 13 The Lord stood above it and said, "I am the Lord God of Abraham your father and the God of Isaac. The land on which you lie, to you will I give it and to your descendants. 14 Your descendants will be like the dust of the earth, and you will spread abroad to the west and to the east and to the north and to the south, and in you and in your descendants, all the families of the earth will be blessed. 15 Remember, I am with you, and I will protect you wherever you go, and I will bring you back to this land. For I will not leave you until I have done what I promised you."

In a different encounter, God uses an angel God to wrestle with Jacob. It is an important encounter because Jacob perseveres and through it his name is changed to Israel. He becomes the founder of the nation of Israel.

Genesis 32: 24 Jacob was left alone, and a man wrestled with him there until daybreak. 25 When the man saw that He did not prevail against Jacob, He touched the socket of his thigh, so the socket of Jacob's thigh was dislocated, as he wrestled with Him. 26 Then He said, "Let Me go, for the day breaks."

But Jacob said, "I will not let You go, unless You bless me."

27 So He said to him, "What is your name?"

And he said, "Jacob."

28 Then the man said, "Your name will no more be called Jacob, but Israel. For you have fought with God and with men, and have prevailed."

God speaks to Joseph through dreams. Joseph doesn't pray for the interpretation and unwisely tells it to his brothers but he is sure God has given him the dream.

God appears to Moses in the burning bush as a bright shining light. He appears as a bright light. He speaks with Moses in this particular way so that Moses knows he has encountered God.

Exodus 3: 2 The angel of the Lord appeared to him in a flame of fire from the midst of a bush, and he looked, and the bush burned with fire, but the bush was not consumed. 3 So Moses said, "I will now turn aside and see this great sight, why the bush is not burnt."

4 When the Lord saw that he turned aside to see, God called to him from out of the midst of the bush and said, "Moses, Moses."

God manifests Himself through miracles with Moses and Israel. He also covers them or protects them by supernatural occurrences.

Exodus 13: 21 The Lord went before them by day in a pillar of cloud to lead them along the way, and by night in a pillar of fire, to give them light, so that they might travel by day and by night. 22 He did not remove the pillar of cloud by day or the pillar of fire by night from before the people.

Even though God spoke with Moses regularly and manifested Himself in many miracles, Moses wanted to see God's glory. God causes His glory to pass behind Moses but instructs Him that no person can see God's glory and live.

Exodus 33: 18 Then Moses said, "I pray, show me Your glory."

19 Then He said, "I will make all My goodness pass before you, and I will proclaim the name of the Lord before you. I will be gracious to whom I will be gracious and will show mercy on whom I will show mercy." 20 He said,

"You cannot see My face, for no man can see Me and live."

Mostly God sent angels who appeared in the form of men to speak with prophets as they did with Abraham (Genesis 18: 2) . Some occasions, God sent angels who appeared without human form as the prophet Ezekiel saw tremendous beautiful fascinating creatures. (Ezekiel 1: 13). Other occasions, God appeared to people in their dreams. Most often he used angels. There are many other occasions where God spoke to people through His servants the Prophets.

It is only in the birth of Jesus Christ, that God appears to people in human form. It is evident in his miraculous birth, the life, death, burial and resurrection of Christ in a glorified body.

2 Corinthians 4: 6 For God, who commanded the light to shine out of darkness, has shone in our hearts to give the light of the knowledge of the glory of God in the face of Jesus Christ.

Jesus appears to the Apostle John on Patmos.

Revelation 1: 12 I turned to see the voice that spoke with me. And when I turned, I saw seven golden candlesticks, 13 and in the midst of the seven candlesticks was one like a Son of Man, clothed with a garment down to the feet and with a golden sash wrapped around the chest. 14 The hair on His head was white like wool, as white as snow. His eyes were like a flame of fire. 15 His feet were like fine brass, as if refined in a furnace, and His voice as the sound of many waters. 16 He had in His right hand seven stars, and out of His mouth went a sharp two-edged sword. His appearance was like the sun shining brightly.

Jesus appearance is so bright and glorious that John falls at his feet. Even though he was in his glorified human body, his glory was overwhelming. Even though it was a vision, it was too much for a human being to receive.

I have given these examples of God speaking with people as example of God making Himself known to people for thousands of years yet none of those people made an image of God or worshipped any idol.

Those mentioned in the Bible who sinned against God by making idols are many. Moses and Aaron were used by God to do mighty miracles in Egypt so that Israel would be set free. Aaron is with Moses as these mighty miracles occur. As Moses is on Mount Sinai speaking to God and receiving the commandments, Israel sins horribly as they are waiting for Moses return. The people complained and grumbled about Moses being gone so long.

Aaron commits a horrible sin:

Exodus 32: 2 Aaron said to them, "Break off the gold earrings that are in the ears of your wives, your sons, and your daughters, and bring them to me." 3 So all the people broke off the gold earrings that were in their ears and brought them to Aaron. 4 He received them from their hand, and fashioned it with an engraving tool, and made it into a molded calf. Then they said, "This is your god, O Israel, who brought you up from the land of Egypt."

5 When Aaron saw it, he built an altar before it. And Aaron made a proclamation and said, "Tomorrow will be a feast to the Lord." 6 So they rose up early on the next day, and offered burnt offerings, and brought peace offerings. And the people sat down to eat and to drink, and rose up to play.

Aaron builds an idol and blasphemes God by saying the image is of God. The people wanted to worship an idol because that is what they witnessed around them for 400 years in bondage in Egypt. The Egyptians had many gods and idols of them all throughout the land. Even though the Israelites knew God would deliver them, they had been polluted by the idol worshippers around them. It influenced them.

Jeroboam commits a horrible sin against God not because he believed in the idols but because he wanted to stop the people from worshipping God at Jerusalem. He starts his own pagan religion with bulls. It affected the people of Israel for many years afterwards. The sin is compounded because he swayed all the people in his realm to worship idols for generations beyond his own.

1 Kings 12: 26 Jeroboam said in his heart, "The kingdom will return to the house of David. 27 If this people go up to do sacrifice in the house of the Lord at Jerusalem, then shall the heart of this people turn again to their lord, even to Rehoboam king of Judah, and they shall kill me and go again to Rehoboam king of Judah."

28 At that point, the king got some advice and made two golden calves and said to the people, "It is too difficult for you to go up to Jerusalem. Here are your gods, O Israel, which brought you up out of the land of Egypt." 29

He set one in Bethel, and he put the other in Dan. 30 This was a sin, for the people went to worship before the one, even all the way in Dan.

God commands Moses not to worship idols or to let the people worship any man-made thing or anything that God has made. This warning was special because all the land that Israel would inherit was inhabited by idol worshippers.

Deuteronomy 4: 15 Give good care to yourselves, for you saw no form on the day that the Lord spoke to you in Horeb from the midst of the fire, 16 lest you corrupt yourselves and make a graven image for yourselves in the form of any figure, the likeness of male or female, 17 the likeness of any beast that is on the earth, the likeness of any winged fowl that flies in the air, 18 the likeness of anything that creeps on the ground, the likeness of any fish that is in the waters beneath the earth. 19 And beware, lest you lift up your eyes to heaven, and when you see the sun, and the moon, and the stars, even all the host of heaven, you are led astray and worship them, and serve them, that which the Lord your God has allotted to all nations under the whole heaven. 20 But the Lord has taken you and brought you out of the iron furnace, from Egypt, to be to Him a people of inheritance, as you are today.

Israel was strictly forbidden to worship idols and given a commandment to kill idol worshippers and never marry an idol worshipper.

God continuously warns Israel not to bow down or worship any idol or image, All of the nations they will inherit and possess were filled with idol worshippers.

Deuteronomy 30: 17 But if your heart turns away, so that you do not obey, but are drawn away, and worship other gods and serve them, 18 then I declare to you today that you will surely perish and that you will not prolong your days in the land which you are crossing the Jordan to go in and possess.

Moses instruction with many of the idol worshippers was to completely kill all of them. They were not to marry them or to take them in as slaves. In one instance, a man of Israel, takes an idol worshipper in as a wife and brings a plague upon all of the Israelites because of God's wrath.

Exodus 23: 23 For My angel will go before you and bring you to the Amorites, and the Hittites, and the Perizzites, and the Canaanites, the Hivites, and the Jebusites, and I will completely destroy them. 24 You must not bow down to their gods, or serve them, or do according to their practices, but you shall utterly overthrow them and break down their images in pieces.

Numbers 25: Moses said to the judges of Israel, "Kill each of the men who have aligned themselves with the Baal of Peor."

6 Behold, one of the children of Israel came and brought to his brothers a Midianite woman in the sight of Moses and in the sight of all the assembly of the children of Israel, who were weeping before the door of the tent of meeting. 7 When Phinehas the son of Eleazar, the son of Aaron the priest, saw it, he rose up from among the assembly and took a spear in his hand, 8 and he went after the man of Israel into the tent, and thrust both of them through, the man of Israel and the woman through her belly. So the plague was stopped from the children of Israel. 9 Those that died in the plague were twenty-four thousand.

There are religions today that still worship idols. There are well meaning people who worships pictures of Jesus or Mary. There are people who worship artifacts of Christianity. Although it is right to be respectful to artifacts from the Bible, no one knows what Jesus really looked like. The Shroud of Turin is our closest clue, if in fact it is authentic. Even should it truly be the burial shroud of Christ, we must not worship it. Anything that man could create can never be God. Anything that God has created can never be God.

If a people is given to idol worship, that sin can become an iniquity. What that means is people get hard towards the real God and pleasure in the sin. The curse of worshipping idols is losing all of the blessings promised to those who worship the One true God – Jehovah. It is forbidden to worship anything that represents God because God is Omnipotent, Omnipresent, Omniscient and Almighty. There is nothing that can accurately represent God.

If there is some object or picture or thing that you worship, you must get rid of it. I was not raised in a Christian home and I had collected many things from different religions, mostly books, jewelry etc. After being a Christian for one day, the Holy Spirit within me prompted me to burn many books. Also, I knew I had to get rid of pictures of idols and jewelry made for idols. O person instructed me. God's Spirit on the inside of me instructed me. I knew it was necessary.

Keeping a statue or a picture of an idol or books about an idol is forbidden. Any area of disobedience to God, is an entrance point for Satan and the demons.

Often people use the term "idol" to mean hero or favourite sports' star or singer. I myself had special people who were my heroes. What can happen to some people, not many but enough that it is noticeable is that they give too much of their focus to famous people, or idols or heroes. There are people who become obsessed so that they collect pictures, items, etc. of people. There are such people who plagued Elvis Presley. There are such people who plagued Michael Jackson. There are such people who will follow and hunt for superstars or idols in an unnatural way. It is not wrong to admire people, but first, God must be God in your life. If a person gets too obsessed about his or her idol, he or she can become bothersome to the idol. It could end in death as with John Lennon being stalked by a worshipper. I only mention this is a caution. The caution is that a person, or a sports team, or anything on earth could be magnified beyond its importance and become and idol to someone.

If we truly worship God, we will desire to obey His Word; we will not worship anything or anyone but God. After the resurrection, Jesus reveals himself to the disciples in the upper room that they celebrated Passover in. Thomas was not there. Although all the disciples tell them they have seen Jesus Resurrected, Thomas has words of prove it to me or I won't believe – a negative attitude about believing. Once Thomas sees the resurrected LORD appear with the nail prints in his hands and feet and pierced wound in His side, Thomas believes and exclaims "My Lord and my God". Jesus doesn't condemn him but rather exhorts those who never see Jesus to still believe. Believing on the LORD Jesus Christ requires faith. There are millions of Christians who do not personally encounter Jesus face to face but believe because God's word is true and it pierces their hearts so they can believe and be saved.

John 20: But he said to them, "Unless I see the nail prints in His hands, and put my finger in the nail prints, and put my hand in His side, I will not believe."

26 After eight days His disciples were again inside with the doors shut, and Thomas was with them. Jesus came and stood among them, and said, "Peace be with you." 27 Then He said to Thomas, "Put your finger here, and look at My hands. Put your hand here and place it in My side. Do not be faithless, but believing."

28 Thomas answered Him, "My Lord and my God!"

29 Jesus said to him, "Thomas, because you have seen Me, you have believed. Blessed are those who have not seen, and have yet believed."

We honour God with worship and praise and our faith in him. Jesus explains that it is spiritual. It is not a physical religion or duty. It is a spiritual encounter. You do not worship a picture or a statue of God. You worship the One true God with your spirit directly communicating with the Holy Spirit.

John 4: 24 God is Spirit, and those who worship Him must worship Him in spirit and truth."

4 CHAPTER

3rd Commandment
4th Commandment

Deuteronomy 5: 11 You shall not take the name of the Lord your God in vain, for the Lord will not exonerate anyone who takes His name in vain.

The language we use matters. The words we say impact the listener. They can bring encouragement, comfort, inspiration, joy. They can be like darts that pierce someone. They could release negative feelings and impact the listener for evil. This topic itself is worthy of a detailed study. It is important to know that our words matter.

Proverbs 18: 1 Death and life are in the power of the tongue,
and those who love it will eat its fruit.

Words we speak impact three realms of beings:

1. Yourself
2. Others
3. Spirit realm

Words and their impact in these realms is sown throughout the Bible scriptures. The Psalmists often pray that their words and their lives would align with God's word. Only when both our words and our lives agree with God's Word are we truly living it.

Psalm 19: 14 Let the words of my mouth and the meditation of my heart
be acceptable in Your sight,
O Lord, my strength and my Redeemer.

God warns us about the words we speak. It is a hard saying but Jesus tells us we will give account for every word we speak. What that means is we should be careful about the words we speak selecting the correct precise words and not exaggerating or speaking in a tone that we would regret. I am especially aware of this scripture because God has quickened it to me often because of my profession as a teacher. Teachers can say words to build up and encourage their students. An angry word or insult from a teacher can impact a person lifelong. It is because we highly regard teachers as those who help to shape people's lives. As a teacher I am entrusted with much responsibility that can directly affect people's lives.

Matthew 12: 36 But I say to you that for every idle word that men speak, they will give an account on the Day of Judgment. 37 For by your words you will be justified, and by your words you will be condemned."

Often, the words we speak to ourselves and about ourselves is not always exact. Some people make jokes about themselves as a way of humour that insults themselves. You may consider this harmless fun but in reality, what you say about yourself, you are speaking over self as a kind of prophetic direction. Some people, are hard on themselves; perhaps more than on any other people. It is a trait of a leader to expect himself or herself to do the best. If the person makes an error, the person may insult himself or herself. It is good to aim for perfection and excellence, but saying negative words about yourself, are as seeds being planted into your ears and heart. If you speak negative words and your spirit receives them, what you will be doing is polluting the good soil of your heart with wicked words, nasty words, insulting words etc.

It is important for all people, even the perfectionist leaders to admit an error and at once receive the inspiration to improve. It would be good to reflect on what was done incorrectly and how it could be improved. Rather than complain, let your spirit man command your soul to come into order. Let the creative, inspired, spiritual you speak with God and get a solution or series of alternatives so that you will not make the same error again.

Speak to yourself words of encouragement. Give yourself the chances of mercy that you would give to a friend or respected colleague. I learned this kind of attitude through my life of being involved in sports and athletics. I was competitive always, striving to do my best. I don't like to lose. I hate losing. I have a positive perspective though; I realize where mistakes were made, encourage myself and others and get ready for the next event with a positive attitude. As, I became a Christian, I realized God cared about my attitude towards myself, others and all those at the sports' event. I've had some excellent coaches who taught me, encouraged me, used me, helped me to develop in my skills, knew my skills etc. That has all influenced me to want to help others in a similar way through my teaching.

As we speak words, we get what we say.

I know it seems hard to believe but let us take it literally. If I go to McDonald's and order a Whopper, there is no way I am going to get it. They don't sell them there. I ask for a Combo number and get a Big Mac and fries and a pop. You get what you ask for. Any store you go to, if you do not ask correctly, you will not get the desired result. If you are saying words that insult yourself or others, you are going to reap what you are sowing with your words.

Mark 11: 24 Therefore I say to you, whatever things you ask when you pray, believe that you will receive them, and you will have them.

It isn't always easy to speak what you want to receive.. I know it from athletics; God taught it to me. I reap what I sow; Should I speak words of winning, excellence, aiming for perfection, aiming to do my personal best. This covers athletic skill, encouraging my soul and being a partner with the Holy Spirit, receiving strength from God who quickens me. I can call into existence what never existed before. I can do my best and aim to surpass my person best. I do it regularly. Aim for excellence.

If the situation requires something that never existed before, speak that it will be supplied.

That is what Abraham did. He was 90 years old. His wife was also old. God promised Abraham that he would have children and that his descendants would be as numerous as the stars in the sky. It seems ridiculous to believe God's promise at the age of 90, but Abraham did. His name had been Abram and God gave him a new name Abraham – meaning he would have a multitude of children. Each time someone said his name, it was calling into being the things that God had promised but had not yet manifested.

Romans 4: 16 Therefore the promise comes through faith, so that it might be by grace, that the promise would be certain to all the descendants, not only to those who are of the law, but also to those who are of the faith of Abraham, who is the father of us all 17 (as it is written, "I have made you a father of many nations"[c]) before God whom he believed, and who raises the dead, and calls those things that do not exist as though they did.

Romans 4: 17 (as it is written, "I have made you a father of many nations"[c]) before God whom he believed, and who raises the dead, and calls those things that do not exist as though they did.

Believe for the best. Do your best. Aim to surpass all person bests. As long as you are living aim for the best. Speak words that encourage yourself in each area of your life.

Words we say to others

Words we speak to others are really important. So many children I have known have had a parent or teacher say negative things to them and they believed those things. They accept an "I can't" attitude about certain areas of their lives. Parents must be careful about the words they speak to their children. The words a family member speaks over you can cause you to rise to have confidence and strong self-esteem. Words can also not only wound but scar people. Only God can heal those types of situations.

Ephesians 6: 4 Fathers, do not provoke your children to anger, but bring them up in the discipline and instruction of the Lord.

Jesus strictly kept all the laws of Moses without sin. He lived a holy life. Jesus spoke words of judgement prophetically over some religious people who were hypocrites. Jesus did not speak condemning words to sinners. He offered sinners a way for forgiveness. Jesus warned us not to speak foolishly or with foul words or cursing.

Matthew 5: 22 But I say to you that whoever is angry with his brother without a cause shall be in danger of the judgment. And whoever says to his brother, 'Raca,' shall be in danger of the Sanhedrin. But whoever says, 'You fool,' shall be in danger of hell fire.

We should not use any insulting words as jokes to people. Behind the laughter is a critical spirit. Curse words towards people is exactly what it says. The cursing person is cursing the person. He or she is sowing seeds of damnation or condemnation at the person. Not only does it send negative words, thought, feelings towards the person, because it is a sin, you are sinning against yourself and God. As you release cursing, you are directly going against God's word.

The origin of profanities can be traced to Adam and Eve after they sinned. God questions Adam and Eve because they have covered themselves with leaves and are trying to hide from God. God questions them. Rather than accept responsibility for their sin they blame each other and the serpent. This blaming of others brings judgement from God.

Genesis 3: 12 The man said, "The woman whom You gave to be with me, she gave me fruit of the tree, and I ate."

13 Then the Lord God said to the woman, "What have you done?"

And the woman said, "The serpent deceived me, and I ate."

Cursing is forbidden. We are to speak words that build up, encourage, exhort and teach. If someone does something that makes you angry, rather than say negative words, go somewhere else and let your temper cool before you say anything. If you speak angry words harshly, you may cause strife. Strife is the enemy because it brings division and negative things result from it.

If you have not read John Bevere's book on the Bait of Satan, I would highly recommend it. Also, Joyce Meyer has a book on Life Without Strife. Those are excellent examples of books about preventing strife and bringing peace to communications.

Words you would have blurted out in anger can be totally changed as you let your spirit lead your soul and you speak words that are true, express your opinion but without malice or negativity. I have not seen it except in movies, but often there is a bomb that is set to go off, and someone is trying to stop it by taking it apart. The person is successful and the bomb threat is gone. No danger. If the person cannot do it, the bomb goes off killing, destroying and damaging (John 10: 10). The enemy uses negative words to break up families, relationships, friendships.

Many marriages could be saved, if people would vow to let no strife in their marriage.

Proverbs 15:
A soft answer turns away wrath,
  but grievous words stir up anger.

I am a teacher; in reality, I am paid to speak for a living. I talk about things I've learned so that others may learn those things. Most teachers love to talk. Most teachers will tell you every possible detail about what they know. What is important is that we also be listeners. We should not speak just to speak. In our jobs, we should be careful about what we say to students. In our private lives, we should speak if it is important. We should care about people enough to listen to them.

I've had people, who are no longer in my life, dump on me. What that means is the person talks as though his or her mouth is a stream of nonsense. The words pour out. They may be positive. They may be negative. The person is dumping. It means the person doesn't really care about what you have to say or what you think but the person wants to release a stream of garbage. Those people have no care over their words. I would compare it to dirty water that flows with anything and everything in it. We should speak only if it can add to the relationship. If in any way we don't care what we say to the person we are talking to, we are dumping on them. It isn't right. It means we do not honour them enough to care to talk and converse with them.

Proverbs 15

2 The tongue of the wise uses knowledge aright,
but the mouth of fools pours out foolishness.

Blasphemy: Cursing God

Curse words of any type are wrong but it is blasphemy to take the LORD God's name in vain. It means that you could be cursing God. It means that you could be lying in an oath swearing to tell the truth while you are lying. If you give and oath promising to tell the truth in God's name but do not tell the truth, it is a sin. If you take a vow, a solemn promise to do something in God's name but do not do it, it is a sin. It means that you are directly abusing the name of the LORD. It is a sin. A vow to God must be honoured. It must be kept. If you do not keep your promise to God, it is a sin. The scripture warns us not to lightly say vows.

Some people curse so much, it is hard for them to speak without curse words. I have known those types of people. None of those people are in my life. Using profanity is a sin because we are to live in the spirit, speak words on purpose to convey thoughts and feelings. If a person grows up in a home where there is much cursing, most likely that person will also do the same. If a person continues to curse and does not stop, the person may get a cursing spirit. A demonic spirit can attach itself to a person who continuously curses. The only help that can come to these people is salvation, deliverance and aligning himself or herself to God's Word.

Christians are to live in the Spirit.

Galatians 5: 16 I say then, walk in the Spirit, and you shall not fulfill the lust of the flesh. 17 For the flesh lusts against the Spirit, and the Spirit against the flesh. These are in opposition to one another, so that you may not do the things that you please.

Galatians 5: 25 If we live in the Spirit, let us also walk in the Spirit.

The words we say, pray, confess and profess directly affect us, the people in our lives and the realm of the spirit. As our words align with God's word, we live Holy. God releases angels to protect us as we align with His word. If we speak negative things over ourselves, people or God, and we do not repent we directly affect the spirit realm.

If you are a Christian and you know that you curse but thought it was just a bad habit, please be serious about repenting and asking god to cleanse you and help you to speak words of life rather than cursing. If you know you cannot stop yourself, maybe you tried, but cannot stop it, you must repent and commit yourself wholly unto God.

1 Thessalonians 5: 23 May the very God of peace sanctify you completely. And I pray to God that your whole spirit, soul, and body be preserved blameless unto the coming of our Lord Jesus Christ. 24 Faithful is He who calls you, who also will do it.

There are many ministries with excellent teaching on the words we speak and their impact. I highly recommend these authors: Joyce Meyer, Kenneth Copeland, Jerry Savelle, Joel Osteen, Jesse Duplantis. There are many others. If you do not have any of their books on words or the mouth, please get them and invest into yourself because your words impact you; your words impact the people around you' your words impact the spirit realm.

Casually using God's name

Do not use God's name, if you do not mean it. I myself picked up a habit of saying "O God" as a pause in a conversation or to affirm that I could relate to someone was saying. It was wrong. Do not say "God" if you don't mean it. It is using God's name casually and without reverence or respect. Many Jews and Messianic Jews so highly respect God that they will not even write the word "God" they will place only part of the letters such as G-d They honour and respect using God's name.

The Forth commandment

4th Deuteronomy 5: 12 Keep the Sabbath day, to keep it holy, just as the Lord your God has commanded you. 13 Six days you shall labor and do all

your work, 14 but the seventh day is the Sabbath of the Lord your God. On
it you shall not do any work: you, nor your son, nor your daughter, nor your
male servant, nor your female servant, nor your ox, nor your donkey, nor
any of your livestock, nor the foreigner that is within your gates, so that
your male servant and your female servant may rest as well as you. 15
Remember that you were a servant in the land of Egypt, and that the Lord
your God brought you out from there with a mighty hand and by an
outstretched arm; therefore your God commanded you to keep the Sabbath
day.

God's commandment to keep the sabbath day as a special day holy unto God may seem strange because it commands a day of rest and worship. It is also a command that the servants and animals get a day of rest. Certainly, God is setting an example for us in the creation of all things. God created all things within a 6 day plan. The way God measures day is most certainly not the same as humans do. The scripture states that a thousand human years are as a day to God (2 Peter 3:8). The part I emphasize is that God Himself rested on the 7th day. I don't believe he did it without purpose. God has set an example for us by showing us the 7th day is to worship and rest from work.

Genesis 2: So the heavens and the earth, and all their hosts, were finished.

2 On the seventh day God completed His work which He had done, and
He rested on the seventh day from all His work which He had done. 3
Then God blessed the seventh day and made it holy, because on it He had
rested from all His work which He had created and made.

Making the day Holy means, God set it apart from all the other days; it is different. He commands Israel to remember their captivity in Egypt where they worked as slaves. A day of rest is a special blessing for Israel. It is a special reward from God Himself who set Israel free so that she could worship God and remember God that 7the day especially.

The physical fact is that those who work hard as unto God in their other 6 days require a day of rest. It is a day of refreshing. It is a day where one doesn't have to run around and squeeze things into a schedule. When I was a child, all stores and shopping centers were closed on Sundays. It is only within the last 30 years that it changed. People could not even play baseball in public school yards on a Sunday. It was to be a day of rest. In our fast-paced society, with a strong emphasis on profit and gaining as much money as possible, in North America, our society no longer keeps the Sabbath day. Sure, there are Christian families who do, but many do not;

they use the day to work extra or for hobbies. Many people use it as a family day.

The truth is that the Jewish Sabbath day is a Saturday not a Sunday. We Christians celebrate Jesus Christ's resurrection on a Sunday so most church services are on a Sunday and it is the day we purpose to keep as a Sabbath. The important aspect is that there should be a day of rest as well as remembering of the LORD, a day of worship. God is pretty strict about it. You may think it is optional, but it is a commandment. It is for our health and wellbeing. It brings refreshment and renewal to the human body. It gives families a chance to worship God together. It gives us a chance to connect with other people of like precious faith (2 Peter 1: 1).

God taught Israel by example

God supernaturally supplied manna or bread from heaven each day for the Israelites for 6 days in each week. At the end of each day they were to collect as much as necessary, not hoard it because it would get mushy and filled with worms after one day. God was showing Israel how to rely on God for provision. Israel had to obey God or they would not be within the sphere of blessing. On the 6th day though, they were commandment to collect twice as much as before so they would have provision for the sabbath day. They were forbidden to collect manna on the 7th day as it was to be a day of rest from all work and also a day of remembering and honouring the LORD.

Exodus 16: 4 Then the Lord said to Moses, "Indeed, I will rain bread from heaven for you. And the people shall go out and gather a certain amount every day, that I may test them, whether they will walk in My law or not. 5 And it shall come to pass that on the sixth day they shall prepare that which they bring in, and it will be twice as much as they gather daily."

The people heard the commandments of God but not all the people obeyed. Some tried to hoard the manna and keep it overnight. It became mushy and filled with worms. Some people ignored the command not to collect manna on the 7th day and they found nothing. God Himself did not give them manna on the 7th day. Rather, God instructed them, commanded them to collect on the 6th day and rest on the 7th day.

Exodus 16: 21 So they gathered it every morning, every man according to what he could eat. And when the sun got hot, it melted. 22 Now on the sixth day they gathered twice as much bread, two omers[b] per man, and then all the leaders of the congregation came and told Moses. 23 He said to them, "This is what the Lord has said, 'Tomorrow is the Sabbath, a holy Sabbath to the Lord. Bake that which you will bake today, and boil that you will boil, and all that which remains over lay up for yourselves to be kept until the morning.' "

Exodus 16: 27 It happened that some of the people went out on the seventh day to gather, but they found nothing. 28 Then the Lord said to Moses, "How long will you refuse to keep My commandments and My instructions? 29 See, the Lord has given you the Sabbath; therefore He gives you bread for two days on the sixth day. Every man remain in his place. Let no man go out of his place on the seventh day." 30 So the people rested on the seventh day.

Commanded to Remember God

Israel was commanded to remember the mighty miracles that God did to set Israel free. They were to tell the things of their history to their children and their families. The Levites were consecrated unto God to teach the laws of God to the people and to make the meaning clear to them. It is from this command to remember God and teach the words of God to our families that we developed the synagogue and the Christian Church. We gather to remember our God and to remember what things He has taught us. The Israelites had no written scripture except for the words of God that God Himself carved into stone tablets. God revealed to Moses many aspects of human life and gave Moses a total of 613 laws and commandments. The Levites were to be wholly consecrated or separated unto God for service to God. They were chosen by God specifically to worship and care for all the things and matters of worship.

On the 7th day, they were to gather together as a people who would worship and praise God and remember the greatness of God towards them. God commanded them to remember.

Deuteronomy 11: 11 You must love the Lord your God and keep His charge, His statutes, His ordinances, and His commandments always. 2 Know this day that I am not speaking with your children who have not known and who have not seen the discipline of the Lord your God, His greatness, His mighty hand, and His outstretched arm, 3 and His signs and His works which He did in the midst of Egypt to Pharaoh, the king of Egypt, and to all his land, 4 and what He did to the army of Egypt, to their horses, and to their chariots, when He made the water of the Red Sea to flow over them as they pursued after you, and how the Lord utterly destroyed them, 5 and what He did to you in the wilderness until you came to this place, 6 and what He did to Dathan and Abiram, the sons of Eliab, the son of Reuben, when the earth opened its mouth and swallowed them up, their households, their tents, and everything that was in their possession, in the midst of all Israel. 7 But your eyes have seen all the great deeds of the Lord which He did.

God promised to bless them who would harken to His commandments and obey Him.

Deuteronomy 11: 13 It will be, if you will diligently obey My commandments which I am commanding you today, to love the Lord your God, and to serve Him with all your heart and with all your soul, 14 then I will give you the rain of your land in its season, the early rain and the latter rain, that you may gather in your grain and your wine and your oil. 15 I will provide grass in your fields for your livestock, that you may eat and be full.

They were taught by God how to live a holy life. They were to remember God's word. Some Jewish people literally put boxes to hold scripture on their foreheads and on their hands. These are called phylacteries. It is a physical representation to help them remember their God. Also they were commanded to write the word of God on their doorposts and their homes. Many Jewish people still do have Mezuzahs, containers with scriptures in it on their doorways. It reminds them of God. Judaism was not created by man. Judaism started by God instructing Moses to instruct Israel in what was pleasing to God and right from wrong. God gave Moses all of the plans to build the tabernacle of worship. God taught Israel how to worship so it was pleasing to God.

Deuteronomy 11: 18 Therefore you must fix these words of mine in your heart and in your soul, and bind them as a sign on your hand, so that they may be as frontlets between your eyes. 19 You shall teach them to your children, speaking of them when you sit in your house and when you walk by the way, when you lie down, and when you rise up. 20 You shall write them on the doorposts of your house and on your gates, 21 so that your days and the days of your children may be multiplied in the land which the Lord swore to your fathers to give them, as long as the days of heaven on the earth.

The reward for worshipping God includes blessings in all area of life: health, long life, prosperity, fertility, abundance, more than enough of all things that people could need or want on earth. It gives God pleasure to bless his people so they are completely joyful in all areas of life. The list of blessings for Israel include all areas of life. It covers all aspects of human life possible. Blessing means more than enough. It means never lacking or doing without. Here is a list of blessings God promised Israel.

Deuteronomy 28: 1 Now it will be, if you will diligently obey the voice of the Lord your God, being careful to do all His commandments which I am commanding you today, then the Lord your God will set you high above all the nations of the earth. 2 And all these blessings will come on you and overtake you if you listen to the voice of the Lord your God.
3 You will be blessed in the city and blessed in the field.
4 Your offspring will be blessed, and the produce of your ground, and the offspring of your livestock, the increase of your herd and the flocks of your sheep.
5 Your basket and your kneading bowl will be blessed.
6 You will be blessed when you come in and blessed when you go out.
7 The Lord will cause your enemies who rise up against you to be defeated before you; they will come out against you one way and flee before you seven ways.
8 The Lord will command the blessing on you in your barns and in all that you set your hand to do, and He will bless you in the land which the Lord your God is giving you.

God promised to pour out all types of blessings upon His covenant people. His covenant people would keep all of the commandments and honour God in the ways that god instructed Moses to instruct the Israelites. Part of the blessing they inherited is that they would be a special people, particular to God and they would not be ensnared by false idols or false religions or entangled in sins and iniquities. They were chosen to be a Holy People.

Deuteronomy 28: 12 The Lord will open up to you His good treasure, the heavens, to give the rain to your land in its season and to bless all the work of your hand. You will lend to many nations, but you will not borrow. 13
The Lord will make you the head and not the tail; you will only be above and you will not be beneath, if you listen to the commandments of the Lord your God, which I am commanding you today, to observe and to do them.
14 Also, you shall not turn aside from any of the words which I am commanding you today, to the right hand or to the left, to go after other gods to serve them.

The only way those laws and commandments and the history of what God had done for them as a people could be imparted to the Israelites is by them receiving a day of rest from work and devoting it to learn about God and to worship God. That day of rest is a day of worship.

Nehemiah

After Solomon's Temple was destroyed and the Jews were all scattered and living in bondage, God does a miracle. God softens the heart of a pagan king Cyrus, to issue a decree to rebuild the walls of Jerusalem and to let the Israelites go to worship their God. It is an absolute miracle. God heard the people and kept His covenant promise to Solomon that if the Jews had sinned and were scattered throughout the earth, but they repented, God would gather them once again to their home. Nehemiah (a slave to the king) is commissioned to oversee the rebuilding of Jerusalem.

Finally, after the foundation of the temple is built, after the walls of Jerusalem had been erected, Ezra the scribe reads the Word of God to all the people who were gathered unto Jerusalem. The people did not have opportunity or Sabbath rest all their years in captivity. They gather and hear the commandments of God and all the writings of Moses. As the people heard the Word of God, their hearts rejoiced and they shouted " Amen. Amen." They could freely worship their God. Worship was their response. Some wept because of the beauty of God's Word and their freedom to worship once more. The leaders had to encourage the people to rejoice in the day.

Nehemiah 8: 9 Then Nehemiah the magistrate, Ezra the priest and scribe, and the Levites who were teaching the people said to all the people, "This day is holy to the Lord your God. Stop mourning and weeping." (This was because all the people wept when they heard the words of the Law.)

The people were overcome with gratitude and also knowing that some of them did not even know the Words of God. Ezra read the scriptures – explaining the meaning for hours that day. The people stood and lifted their hands and worshipped as the Word of God was read. The priests encouraged the people to rejoice in the day. They were told to celebrate because God was with them. The people rejoiced and celebrated that day of worship given to them once more.

Nehemiah 8: 10 Then he said to them, "Go your way. Eat the fat, drink the sweet drink, and send portions to those for whom nothing is prepared; for this day is holy to our Lord. Do not be grieved, for the joy of the Lord is your strength."
11 So the Levites quieted all the people, saying, "Hush! Because today is holy you should stop being so sorrowful."
12 Then all the people went to eat, to drink, to send portions, and to enjoy

a great celebration because they had understood the words declared to them.

Of course the 7th day was to be restored as a day of rest and worship. The Levites were once more set apart to worship and honour the LORD by teaching the people and keeping all the things regarding sacrifices and offerings as Aaron and the Levites had been chosen by God. Praise and worship was once more a priority.

Nehemiah 12: 44 At that time men were appointed to govern over the chambers for the treasures, for the contributions, for the first fruits, and for the tithes, so that they might gather into them out of the fields of the cities the legal portions belonging to the priests and Levites. This was because the celebration of Judah survived on the basis of the priests and the Levites 45 who, accompanied by the singers and the gatekeepers, attentively preserved the practices of their God and the practices of purification, according to the commandment of David and of his son Solomon. 46 For in the former days of David and Asaph there were leaders for the singers, the songs of praise, and thanksgivings to God.

Worshippers and singers and musicians gave their lives to worship God and to lead the people in corporate worship. Once more God was worshipped as Israel His people gave themselves to God. Even though they were now free, some of them did not align their lives with the words of God's teaching. They were in disobedience to God and Nehemiah saw it and it grieved him to pray and intercede for Israel but also to take action. He witnessed people disobeying the Sabbath commandment. He was so angry, because it was because of a breaking of God's commandments and disobedience to God that caused Israel to be scattered and become as slaves.

Nehemiah 13: 15 In those days I saw in Judah some treading winepresses on the Sabbath or hauling loads of grain or loading donkeys with wine, grapes, figs, and all manner of burdens in order to bring them to Jerusalem on the Sabbath day. So, during the day while they were selling the food goods, I warned them. 16 Men of Tyre also stayed there, having hauled in fish and all kinds of merchandise, and sold them on the Sabbath to the people of Judah, and in Jerusalem. 17 Then I confronted the nobles of Judah and asked them, "What is this evil thing that you are doing, profaning the Sabbath day? 18 Did not your fathers do likewise? Did not our God bring all this evil against us and against this city? Will you yet bring more wrath upon Israel by profaning the Sabbath?"

Not only does Nehemiah reprove or correct those Israelites that were working on the Sabbath day but he also literally stands at the gates of Jerusalem and threatens those who come to buy and sell and do commercial business on the Sabbath day. He threatens them with force if they return. Once more the Sabbath is honoured and given a place of priority by Nehemiah God's servant who impacted all of Jerusalem by his boldness and zeal.

Nehemiah 13: 19 As the gates of Jerusalem began to cast the evening shadow before the Sabbath, I commanded that the gates should be shut, and charged that they should not be opened until after the Sabbath. Some of my servants I stationed at the gates so that there would be no loads brought in on the Sabbath day. 20 Once or twice the merchants and sellers of all kind of merchandise lodged outside Jerusalem. 21 So I warned them and said to them, "Why do you spend the night next to the wall? If you do so again, I will send you away by force." From that time on they stopped coming on the Sabbath. 22 Then I commanded the Levites to purify themselves so that they could come and, as guardians of the gates, sanctify the Sabbath day.

Jesus and the Sabbath

There were religious people who accused Jesus of not honouring the sabbath. This is certainly a terrible crime. Jesus disciples were gathering handfuls of grain as they travelled. The people who accused Jesus were trying to find anything they could to discredit Jesus. The disciples were not working to harvest grain for anybody. They wanted it themselves as food. They were not doing business.

Matthew 12: 12 At that time Jesus went through the grain fields on the Sabbath. And His disciples were hungry and began to pluck the heads of grain and to eat. 2 But when the Pharisees saw it, they said to Him, "Look, Your disciples are doing that which is not lawful to do on the Sabbath!"
3 But He said to them, "Have you not read what David and those who were with him did when he was hungry, 4 how he entered the house of God and ate the ritual bread, which was not lawful for him to eat, neither for those who were with him, but only for the priests? 5 Or have you not read in the law how on the Sabbath the priests in the temple profane the Sabbath, but are blameless? 6 I say to you, in this place there is One who is greater than the temple. 7 If you had known what this meant, 'I desire mercy, and not sacrifice,' you would not have condemned the innocent. 8 For the Son of Man is Lord even of the Sabbath."

Jesus tells them of exceptions that certainly were acceptable because they were life or death situations. The people were not working. King David was running from Saul who was going to kill him. He was given the showbread (only for holy priests) because it was the only thing he and his men could get. Jesus proclaims that the Messiah is Lord of the Sabbath. He is saying He has authority over all other authority. In a different passage, he clarifies with these words:

Mark 2: 27 Then He said to them, "The Sabbath was made for man, and not man for the Sabbath. 28 So the Son of Man is Lord even of the Sabbath."

God created the Sabbath so that man could be refreshed and renewed and strengthened in his worship and praise to God. Jesus also angered the Pharisees when he healed people on the Sabbath day. Jesus was teaching in a synagogue and saw a person who needed healing. He was moved with compassion and healed her. He explains to them they are hypocrites because if an animal of theirs wandered, surely, they would go get it back again. He was pointing to the meaning of the sabbath not being a religious bondage but as day of rest and worship. He states that the woman who had been bound by the devil should certainly be set free as it is God's will to prosper and bless Israel. He is appealing to the Word of God about blessing Israel. Jesus was teaching more than just the Sabbath. He was instructing them how the commandments of God are to be followed by our lives not by a religious tradition.

Luke 13: 10 He was teaching in one of the synagogues on the Sabbath. 11
And there was a woman who had a spirit of infirmity for eighteen years and
was bent over and could not straighten herself up. 12 When Jesus saw her,
He called her and said to her, "Woman, you are loosed from your
infirmity." 13 Then He laid His hands on her, and immediately she was
made straight and glorified God.
14 But the ruler of the synagogue answered with indignation, because Jesus
had healed on the Sabbath, and said to the people, "There are six days in
which men ought to work. Therefore come and be healed on those days,
but not on the Sabbath day."
15 The Lord answered him, "You hypocrite! Does not each one of you on
the Sabbath untie his ox or his donkey from the stall and lead it away to
water it? 16 Then should not this woman, being a daughter of Abraham
whom Satan has bound these eighteen years, be loosed from this bondage
on the Sabbath?"

There Remains a Rest

The writer of Hebrews talks about the issue of rest but in light of Jesus death and burial and resurrection. He points to Jesus as the rest that we enter in. It is faith in Jesus that brings us the rest of the sabbath not just simply not working on the 7th day. Those who have faith, enter into a rest from their own self-righteousness. They are not striving to achieve a place of honour with God but are free because of their faith in Jesus Christ. Because Jesus Christ completely paid the penalty for all sin and unrighteousness, to those who would believe in him, we may enter into the rest of knowing that we are right with God through Jesus Christ. The Sabbath day and rest from physical work is used to teach the people about the spiritual rest that is released to believers in the LORD Jesus Christ. Christians who are living a godly life do not have to try to earn their way or strive to keep all aspect of the law.

Hebrews 4: 4 Therefore, since the promise of entering His rest remains, let
us fear lest any of you should seem to come short of it. 2 For the gospel
was preached to us as well as to them. But the word preached did not
benefit them, because it was not mixed with faith in those who heard it. 3
For we who have believed have entered this rest, as He has said,
"As I have sworn in My wrath,
'They shall not enter My rest.' "[a]
However, His works have been finished since the creation of the world. 4
For He spoke somewhere about the seventh day like this: "And God rested
on the seventh day from all His works."[b] 5 And again in the present
passage He said, "They shall not enter My rest."[c]
6 Since therefore it remains for some to enter it, and they to whom it was
first preached did not enter due to unbelief, 7 again He establishes a certain
day, "Today," saying through David, after so long a time, as it has been
said:
"Today, if you will hear His voice,
do not harden your hearts."[d]

Jesus paid the price for all sins or breaking of the laws. It does not mean we should not honour God or live a pleasing life to God. We should most certainly do our best to live for God. Jesus death, burial and resurrection brought us life. The commandments are important because they express God's will towards man. They instruct us in ways that please God. The blood of Jesus Christ is our salvation – not the keeping of the law. In the past, people who broke any commandment had to offer an animal sacrifice. Jesus is our redeemer. His blood was shed once for all sin.

It is right that we repent if we sin. It is right to accept Jesus blood as redemption and forgiveness from all sin.

John 1: 17 For the law was given through Moses; grace and truth came through Jesus Christ.

5 CHAPTER

5th Commandment

Deuteronomy 5: 16 Honor your father and your mother, just as the Lord your God has commanded you, that your days may be prolonged, and that it may go well with you in the land which the Lord your God is giving you. Exodus 21: 17 He who curses his father or his mother shall surely be put to death.

The commandment to honour parents is unique because with it comes a special promise; If you honour your parents, you will live long. Because it is a conditional blessing, if someone does not honour his parents, long life is not promised. Parents were to love their children and teach them the word of God. Parents were to train them in skills and trades so they could earn a living as well as in all matters concerning living life wholly unto God. It is normal for parents to thank God for their children and to raise their children giving them the best and praying they will accomplish more than the parents. If the parents truly give to their children the best and provide the most excellent example, the children should naturally love their parents.
Proverbs 22: 6 Train up a child in the way he should go,
and when he is old he will not depart from it.

Parents are accountable to raise their children by discovering their gifts and giving them education and training so they can use their gifts. Parents are to live uprightly as worshippers of God giving an example for their children to follow. There are many examples of true parental love for children shown in scripture so that the legacy of faith in one generation, is continued to the next. Abraham who prayed and believed God for a heir who would be multiplied in the earth, finally received the promise of God after more than 30 years. The first thing Abraham does is keep the covenant he has with God. As God commanded, Isaac was circumcised as a sign of Abraham's covenant with God.

Genesis 21: 4 Then Abraham circumcised his son Isaac when he was eight days old, as God had commanded him. 5 Now Abraham was one hundred years old when his son Isaac was born to him.

Abraham gets a wife for Isaac

As Abraham grew near death, he made plans to get a godly wife for Isaac so that Isaac would marry someone who would believe the same. He was keeping his covenant with God because he knew that an ungodly wife could turn the heart of a man to sin and worship idols.

Genesis 24: 24 Now Abraham was old, well advanced in age; and the Lord had blessed Abraham in all things. 2 So Abraham said to his servant, the oldest of his household, who was in charge over all that he had, "Please, place your hand under my thigh, 3 and I will make you swear by the Lord, the God of heaven and the God of the earth, that you will not take a wife for my son from the daughters of the Canaanites, among whom I live. 4 But you shall go to my country and to my family, and take a wife for my son Isaac."

Choosing Rebekah is a promise that the blessing of God will stay upon Abraham's bloodline. God keeps his covenant with Abraham and also appears to Isaac to guide him and direct him in the best possible way and he keeps him from going to Egypt. God renews his promise to Abraham by his covenant continuance on Isaac. God uses the same wording of blessing that he promised to Abraham and pronounces it upon Isaac.

Genesis 26: 2 The Lord appeared to him and said, "Do not go down to Egypt. Live in the land of which I will tell you. 3 Sojourn in this land, and I will be with you and will bless you; for I will give to you and all your descendants all these lands, and I will fulfill the oath which I swore to Abraham your father. 4 I will make your descendants multiply as the stars of the heavens and will give your descendants all these lands. By your descendants all the nations of the earth will be blessed,[a] 5 because Abraham obeyed Me and kept My charge, My commandments, My statutes, and My laws." 6 So Isaac lived in Gerar.

Favouritism perverts the family

Truly there is a blessing or transference of the blessing from one generation to the next. The birth of Isaac's sons are an answer to prayer but the parents' love for their children is divided. The parents have favourites and because of it, there is strife in their home. There is no further explanation for why the parents chose favourites.

Genesis 25: 27 So the boys grew. Esau was a cunning hunter, a man of the field, while Jacob was a calm man, living in tents. 28 Isaac loved Esau, because he ate of his game, but Rebekah loved Jacob.

The effect of favouritism has on the boys is that there becomes an enmity or strife between Esau and Jacob. Jacob deceives Esau and gets his birthright from him. The first born of each family was given high privilege especially concerning matters of inheritance. Esau seems to be a brash character who esteems lightly the promises of God as he sells his God given birthright for a bowl of stew. Later, Rachel's love for Jacob is so strong she schemes with him to trick dying Isaac into giving Jacob the blessings of the first born that would have come through laying on of hands and prayer. Rachel helps Jacob disguise himself as his brother by attaching fur to his arms and neck so that his skin is hard and hairy like Esau. Rachel makes Isaac's favourite type of meat for him and Jacob pretends he caught a deer and prepared it. He lies and says God helped him to catch it (Genesis 27). Isaac falls for the disguise and prays all the blessings he would have prayed over Esau on Jacob. It was a lie and a deception but it still mattered. When Esau comes, Isaac realizes he had been tricked and gives a weak sort of prayer that promises Esau will serve his brother but will finally get free in his later years. Jacob goes to live with family members because Esau is really angry. For years they never see each other.

Their story is like a soap opera. Jacob lives with a scheming uncle who is even more deceitful than himself and he is especially unjust towards his nephew Jacob as he tricks him into 14 years of hard work with the only payment being his daughters as brides. In spite of Jacob's deceptive heart, God prospers him. God's blessing is on him and his wives as it was passed onto him by the laying on of hands through Isaac. The same words of covenant that God promised Abraham are repeated to Jacob. Although he deceived his brother into taking the birthright and the blessing, he gets to keep both.

Genesis 28: 12 He dreamed and saw a ladder set up on the earth with the top of it reaching to heaven. The angels of God were ascending and descending on it. 13 The Lord stood above it and said, "I am the Lord God of Abraham your father and the God of Isaac. The land on which you lie, to you will I give it and to your descendants. 14 Your descendants will be like the dust of the earth, and you will spread abroad to the west and to the east and to the north and to the south, and in you and in your descendants, all the families of the earth will be blessed. 15 Remember, I am with you, and I will protect you wherever you go, and I will bring you back to this land. For I will not leave you until I have done what I promised you."

There are other instances with similar results where one parent chooses one child as a favourite. These are not successful stories of raising a family of faith according to God's plan. Disrespect of parents is a theme that results and there are plenty of stories about disrespect for parents. Perhaps one of the most famous is of Absalom.

Absalom

Ammon, Absalom's brother, rapes his sister Tamar, and then abuses her and tosses her out into the street. Absalom finds her and comforts her and takes her into his home to live with him. King David, should have done something. He is known as a mighty man of God but he did nothing to correct Ammon. What happens as a result is that Absalom schemes against his brother and creates a plan to trap and murder him as revenge for his sister.

David does nothing. He does not reprove him or speak with him. Absalom knows what he has done is a sin. He does not repent for it openly. David's heart longed to see Absalom but he does not send for him. King David was not a good parent. He was not a good example for his children of how to communicate and resolve things. The king's general Joab knew David wanted Absalom to return so he tricks David by sending someone with a false prophetic word to speak with him. David sees through it but still accepts Absalom welcome to return to Jerusalem but not to see him and not to return to his life as part of the family at the palace. That is complete neglect and a breeding ground for Absalom to turn from fearing David to plotting schemes against him. He is angry because David does not communicate directly with him or restore him to his position.

Absalom conspires wickedness

Since he is not given the privileges of a prince, he starts to turn the hearts of the people against David by sowing words of discord or strife into the people who passed by the gate of Jerusalem. He brags about himself as the answer to any problem.

2 Samuel 15: 1 After this Absalom acquired for himself a chariot, horses, and fifty men to run before him. 2 Absalom would go early and stand beside the way into the gate. When any man who had a dispute concerning which he had come to the king for a judgment approached, Absalom would call to him and say, "Which city are you from?" And he would say, "Your servant is from one of the tribes of Israel." 3 Then Absalom would say to him, "Look, your claim is good and right, but there is no one to hear you

on behalf of the king." 4 Absalom would continue, "If I were appointed a judge in the land, then every man who had a claim could come and I would give him justice."

2 Samuel 15: 10 But Absalom sent scouts throughout all of the tribes of Israel, saying, "When you hear the sound of the horn, say: Absalom has become king in Hebron." 11 Now two hundred men went with Absalom from Jerusalem, invited and unsuspecting; they did not know anything. 12 Absalom sent for Ahithophel the Galenite, the advisor of David, from his city Giloh, while he was offering the sacrifices. Now the conspiracy was strong, for the number of people with Absalom was continually growing.

Absalom plotted to overthrow David by rebellion. He gathers and army of people who marched to fight against King David. David could not stay. He feared an over throw of his reign so he abandons his throne. It's almost unbelievable because David was known for being a mighty warrior and for winning hundreds of battles and fights. Rather than fight Absalom head on, David runs away.

2 Samuel 15: 13 A messenger came to David and said, "The hearts of the men of Israel are following Absalom."
14 David said to all of his servants who were with him in Jerusalem, "Get up. We must flee or there will be no escape from Absalom for us. Hurry up and leave, or he will soon reach us and bring disaster upon us, striking the city with the edge of the sword.

Absalom listens to advice to shame and disrespect David in the most personal way. Not only does he come to usurp the throne but he commits wickedness by lying with some of David's wives in public sight of the people.

2 Samuel 16: 21 Ahithophel said to Absalom, "Lie with your father's concubines, whom he left to watch over the palace. When all Israel hears that you have made yourself abhorred by your father, then the hands of all who are with you will be strong." 22 So they set up a tent for Absalom on the roof, and Absalom went in to his father's concubines in the sight of all of Israel.

The defilement of those women was a deliberate act to insult David's authority. His usurping the throne is a result of anger and hatred brooding in him since the rape of his sister. King David gathers an army who fight with him against the army of Absalom. In spite of Absalom's utter wickedness, David commands his captains to deal gently with Absalom. It is parental love but it is ridiculous. They are at war with each other. Joab the general of the army kills Absalom directly disobeying the king. Absalom's pride and selfish desire to usurp power ends in his death while he is the prime of life. If he had been restored to his place in the place and been treated as family rather than as an outcast, he might have inherited a place if authority.

2 Samuel 18: 9 Absalom was encountered by some of the servants of David. Now Absalom was riding on his mule. When the mule went under the branches of a very large tree, his head was caught in the tree. He was left in midair while the mule that was under him kept going.
10 One man saw him and reported it to Joab, saying, "I saw Absalom hanging in a tree."
14 Then Joab said, "I will not waste any more time with you." He took three spears in his hand and thrust them into the heart of Absalom while he
was still alive in the midst of the tree. 15 Then ten young men, armor
bearers for Joab, gathered around and struck down Absalom, killing him.

Honour

Honouring one's parents means to love, respect and treat them with generous kindness. An example of this would be the love that Joseph showed towards Jacob now renamed Israel. Even though Jacob favours Joseph more than his other sons, Joseph keeps his heart kind towards his brothers and forgives them. He is kind and caring towards Israel. Although Joseph has become a mighty man of authority, he personally rides out to welcome his family. He makes arrangements for his family to live in Goshen so they will not be polluted by the idol worship in Egypt itself.

Genesis 46: 29 Joseph readied his chariot and went up to Goshen to meet Israel his father. As soon as he appeared to him, he fell on his neck and wept on his neck a long time.
30 Israel said to Joseph, "Now let me die, since I have seen your face, because you are still alive."
31 Joseph said to his brothers and to his father's household, "I will go up
and tell Pharaoh and say to him, 'My brothers and my father's household,
who were in the land of Canaan, have come to me. 32 The men are
shepherds; their work has been to feed livestock, and they have brought
their flocks and their herds and all that they have.' 33 When Pharaoh calls
you and asks, 'What is your occupation?' 34 you shall say, 'Your servants
have been keepers of livestock from our youth even until now, both we and
our fathers,' so that you may dwell in the land of Goshen, because every
shepherd is an abomination to the Egyptians."

Jesus

Jesus at the age of 12 was in Jerusalem with his parents to worship at the Passover. It was a huge celebration and it is possible they could have been with so many different family members it is possible it would not have been noticed. Joseph and Mary are on their way back to Nazareth when they realize that Jesus is missing. They return to Jerusalem and are of course concerned for their child. They found Jesus preaching in the Temple. His parents question him believing he was disobedient by slipping away from them the way he did.

Luke 2: 47 All who heard Him were astonished at His understanding and
His answers. 48 When they saw Him, they were amazed. And His mother
said to Him, "Son, why have You dealt with us like this? Look, Your father
and I have anxiously searched for You."
49 He said to them, "How is it that you searched for Me? Did you not
know that I must be about My Father's business?" 50 But they did not
understand the word which He spoke to them.
51 Then He went down with them and came to Nazareth and was obedient
to them. But His mother kept all these words in her heart. 52 And Jesus
increased in wisdom and in stature and in favor with God and men.

Please notice, although Jesus does not directly apologize for preaching in the temple, he does submit to them and return to Nazareth. He highly regards his parents as the scripture says he was obedient to them in all things and he increased in wisdom and stature.

Jesus honoured his parents

Jesus respect and care for his mother particularly is shown even from his dying self. Jesus is suffering agony and dying. He sees his mother and the disciple who was his best friend John. They were faithful. They stood at the foot of the cross weeping.

He can see them grieving for him. He speaks words of kind concern for both of them. He cares for his mother and entrust John to care for her for the rest of her life. He knows since they both were closest to him, they will comfort each other.

John 19: 25 But standing by the cross of Jesus were His mother, and His
mother's sister, Mary the wife of Clopas, and Mary Magdalene. 26 When
Jesus saw His mother and the disciple whom He loved standing nearby, He
said to His mother, "Woman, here is your son." 27 Then He said to the

disciple, “Here is your mother.” From that time, this disciple took her to his own home.

Respect of parents

To honour your parents does mean obedience to them, unless they are abusing you or getting you to do illegal things. It seems absurd what I am saying but in our modern school systems, I have known of children who have been physically, sexually and verbally abused by their parents and family members. There are children who are raised by criminals who follow in the paths of their criminal parents. An example of a person who has lived through terrible abuse is Joyce Meyer. She is not just a survivor of abuse. She has victory over abuse through Jesus Christ. She is no longer a victim. If you have not read or heard her testimony, I highly encourage you to listen to it or read it. Although she was severely abused and had tough life, she married a Christian man and gave her self completely to God. God transformed her life completely.

Joyce Meyer

Victims of child abuse often are angry, full of self-pity and self-focus. She lived through those things but is no longer in bondage to those things. She has been completely healed by Jesus Christ. She preaches and teaches and gives her testimony to help women and men who have been abused by encouraging them through the scriptures and her testimonies. Not only is she completely free from all of her childhood abuse, she completely forgave her parents and as she got well known and increased financially, she purchased a new home for her parents.

She assigned people to help them in their elderly years so they could go to appointments and normal things that adult children to assist their elderly parents. She cannot personally be there often because she travels the world preaching Jesus Christ, but she oversaw their care and also got to know that both her parents received Jesus Christ as Saviour before their death. This is truly a story of forgiveness and honouring one’s parents even if one has been harmed by them. The unconditional love of Christ not only healed her but healed their relationship and is being used to change lives because it is a testimony of God’s mercy.

You do not have to agree with your parents. You do not have to obey them in illegal activity or endure abuse, but you must forgive them if they have sinned against you. It is a commandment.

Matthew 6: 14 For if you forgive men for their sins, your heavenly Father will also forgive you. 15 But if you do not forgive men for their sins, neither will your Father forgive your sins.

Forgiving even if you don't feel like it is necessary. Once we obey God and forgive, our hearts are pure. As long as someone holds onto a sin against them or an abuse or any negative things done to you, you are letting that thing become a breeding ground for negative thoughts and wrong heart attitudes. It causes one to focus on himself rather than on God. The person can get bitter and no one wants to be around him of her. Confess that you need a Saviour. Without Jesus forgiving you, you would go to hell. We forgive because Jesus commanded it. If you have any negative feelings about the person, pray a blessing over him or her. You can in faith proclaim 'Jesus I forgive so it is forgiven me'. Jesus can transform your heart so that you may start praying blessings over those people and you may even win them to Christ.

Honouring your parents means caring for them when they can not care for themselves. If the parents can no longer care for themselves physically because of ill health, we should do all we can to help them. It might mean letting them come live with you. It might mean finding a place where they can live life with proper care.

1 Timothy 5: 8 But if any do not care for their own, and especially for those of their own house, they have denied the faith and are worse than unbelievers.

Christian Family

I have mentioned mostly examples of family members who did not properly treat each other according to God's Word. If you were raised in a Christian family, Thank God for them. If your parents prayed for you and gave you the best they could, if your parents imparted truths to you and set a godly example for you, treasure them. Pray for them. Honour them by imparting those same things into your children. There are Christian families today where the parents love and cherish their children, who raise them so that their gifts and talents are developed and so that they honour God first. There are successful families that pass generational blessings from one generation to the next as a legacy.

Deuteronomy 11: 18 Therefore you must fix these words of mine in your heart and in your soul, and bind them as a sign on your hand, so that they may be as frontlets between your eyes. 19 You shall teach them to your children, speaking of them when you sit in your house and when you walk by the way, when you lie down, and when you rise up.

6 CHAPTER

6th commandment

Deuteronomy 5: 17 You shall not murder.

One of the most severe consequences of Adam and Eve`s direct disobedience to God was the murder of Abel by Cain. Hatred and violence are a result of the sin of Adam and Eve. In the excerpt of scripture, Both Cain and Abel bring an offering of sacrifice to God. They give the best they have. One may not understand why God accepted Cain`s sacrifice as pleasing to him while He did not respect the offering of Abel.

Genesis 4: And Abel was a keeper of flocks, but Cain was a tiller of the ground. 3 In the course of time Cain brought an offering to the Lord of the fruit of the ground. 4 Abel also brought the firstborn of his flock and of their fat portions. And the Lord had respect for Abel and for his offering, 5 but for Cain and for his offering, He did not have respect. And Cain was very angry and his countenance fell.

6 The Lord said to Cain, "Why are you angry? Why is your countenance fallen? 7 If you do well, shall you not be accepted?[a] But if you do not do well, sin is crouching at the door. It desires to dominate you, but you must rule over it."

The truth of the scripture can be traced in the origin of sacrifice. Sacrifice is not mentioned before the sin of Adam and Eve. There was no need for a sacrifice because they were living in obedience to God. After Adam and Eve sinned, God made them coats from animal fur. Throughout the remainder of the Old Testament animal sacrifice is made in atonement for sin. It was what God commanded as a penalty for sin. It did not erase the sin, but it covered it until the promised Messiah would come and make atonement for all people.

Genesis 3: 21 The Lord God made garments of skins for both Adam and his wife and clothed them.
Abraham

God makes covenant with Abraham through Abraham`s sacrifice.

God instructed Abraham of what he should do and Abraham obeyed. Abraham prepares the sacrifice. God`s presence came upon him in a dream. God spoke with him about the inheritance he would surely beget. God tells him that his people will be enslaved for 400 years in Egypt before one heir was born. God`s presence consumed the sacrifice. It is from this making of sacrifice that Abraham learns to offer a sacrifice to God. From Abraham to Isaac to Jacob, to Moses etc. sacrifice of animals was the requirement.

Genesis 15: 9 So He said to him, "Bring Me a three-year-old heifer, a three-
year-old female goat, a three-year-old ram, a turtledove, and a young
pigeon."
10 Then Abram brought all of these to Him and cut them in two and laid
each piece opposite the other, but he did not cut the birds in half. 11 When
the birds of prey came down on the carcasses, Abram drove them away.
12 As the sun was going down, a deep sleep fell on Abram, and terror and
a great darkness fell on him. 13 Then He said to Abram, "Know for certain
that your descendants will live as strangers in a land that is not theirs, and
they will be enslaved and mistreated for four hundred years. 14 But I will
judge the nation that they serve, and afterward they will come out with great
possessions. 15 As for you, you will go to your fathers in peace and you will
be buried at a good old age. 16 In the fourth generation, your descendants
will return here, for the iniquity of the Amorites is not yet complete."
17 When the sun went down and it was dark, a smoking fire pot with a
flaming torch passed between these pieces. 18 On that same day the Lord
made a covenant with Abram, saying, "To your descendants I have given
this land, from the river of Egypt to the great Euphrates River— 19 the
land of the Kenites, the Kenizzites, the Kadmonites, 20 the Hittites, the
Perizzites, the Rephaites, 21 the Amorites, the Canaanites, the Girgashites,
and the Jebusites."

Cain`s Anger

Cain`s jealousy of his brother, his rivalry with him caused him to hate his brother. He could have prayed and asked God to show him how to please him. He could have turned to God at that moment to reconcile the situation but instead he became filled with hatred. His anger consumed him. It was so severe he wanted to kill his brother.

Genesis 2: 5 but for Cain and for his offering, He did not have respect. And Cain was very angry and his countenance fell.

God spoke to Cain about his hatred. God warned him. God literally says "If you do well, shall you not be accepted?`` God is speaking with him offering Cain a chance to repent. God is saying that if Cain would make the proper offering, he would be accepted. He also warns him and says if Cain does not repent, if he does not give the right offering, `sin is crouching at the door``. He is warning Cain that if Cain does not turn to God in this moment, he most certainly will commit sin. In God`s mercy, God reached towards Cain, but the hatred in Cain was more than hatred of his brother`s offering. He had enmity or hatred towards God. He was born in sin because of Adam and Eve`s sin. He had in him a hatred towards God.

Genesis 2: 6 The Lord said to Cain, "Why are you angry? Why is your countenance fallen? 7 If you do well, shall you not be accepted?[a] But if you do not do well, sin is crouching at the door. It desires to dominate you, but you must rule over it."

Cain`s hatred turns to the first murder. It is the deliberate willful act of ending someone`s life.

Genesis 2: 8 Cain told Abel his brother. And it came about, when they were in the field, that Cain rose up against his brother Abel and killed him. He showed no sign of repentance, but in fact hardens his heart even more towards God.

God once more speaks with him. God knows what has happened. God is giving a chance for Cain to repent, but he doesn`t. He tries to lie to God rather than admit what he has done.

Genesis 2: 9 The Lord said to Cain, "Where is Abel your brother?"
He said, "I do not know. Am I my brother's keeper?"

Cain`s casual wicked words about not being his brother`s keeper are a lie. He did evil in murdering his brother. He knows it is wrong but hardens his heart and tries to cover it over with a casual tone. Evidently, he had no relationship with God or he would have known that God was Omniscient. God tells him his sin saying that the innocent blood of his brother `cried out` for atonement or justice. Because of Cain's hard heart and evil deed, God places a horrible curse on him. Cain who was in agriculture and harvest is cursed from the land. He is sentenced to wander from place to place.

While many might not believe it is a severe punishment, the truth is if you have enjoyed planting and sowing and reaping, to be deprived of it is a terrible thing; he has lost his first work. It is after this judgement Cain`s heart softens a little. Cain realizes he has lost what he loved and he lost his relationship (of sorts) with God and he is banished and cursed to wander.

He says he cannot bare the judgement. He does not repent. He does not try to plea with God; he does not know God is merciful. His first fear is that someone will kill him. The hatred, the murder releases fear within him that he too might be killed.

Genesis 2: 10 And then He said, "What have you done? The voice of your brother's blood is crying out to Me from the ground. 11 Now you are cursed from the ground which opened its mouth to receive your brother's blood from your hand. 12 From now on when you till the ground, it will not yield for you its best. You will be a fugitive and a wanderer on the earth."

Genesis 2: 13 Then Cain said to the Lord, "My punishment is more than I can bear. 14 You have driven me out this day from the face of the earth, and from your face will I be hidden; and I will be a fugitive and a vagabond in the earth, and it will happen that anyone who finds me will kill me."

God places a special mark on Cain so that anyone who kills him will receive a horrible curse. Cain does not repent. He goes out of the presence of the LORD and lives his life.

Genesis 2: 15 So the Lord said to him, "Therefore whoever kills Cain, vengeance will be taken on him sevenfold." Then the Lord put a mark upon Cain, so that no one finding him would kill him. 16 Then Cain went out from the presence of the Lord and settled in the land of Nod, east of Eden. Because of the sin of murder, not being repented of and not being atoned for, the earth is filled with violence and hatred. Within several generations, the hatred and violence is so severe that God decides to end life on earth as it is. He speaks to Noah and preserves his life. He gets him to take animals with him into the ark and for 120 years Noah warned the people around him that it would rain and that the rain would be a flood that would destroy all life on the earth. Please notice, this is the same type of warning that was given to Cain. A chance to be saved, to find repentance was given them.

Only Noah`s family and the animals entered the ark.

Genesis 6: 11 The earth was corrupt before God and filled with violence. 12 God looked on the earth and saw it was corrupt, for all flesh had corrupted their way on the earth. 13 So God said to Noah, "The end of all flesh is come before Me, for the earth is filled with violence because of them. Now I will destroy them with the earth.

The purpose of this chapter is not to emphasize the Noahic covenant but it must be mentioned because it is the result of violence and murder in the earth. After the animals and Noah`s family enter the ark, the rain comes and covers all the earth. Only those in the ark are saved. Upon the earth drying and becoming inhabitable, Noah`s first response without God even asking for it to is offer a sacrifice to God thanking God for protecting them and preserving them. God commands a blessing on Noah and his family telling them to multiply. It is the same command that God had given to Adam and Eve. God gives him dominion over all the earth. It is the same authority that God had given to Adam and Eve.

God also warns Noah and through him all who would be born after him that blood is special. They are not to eat meat with blood in it. He also announces that there is judgement on anyone who kills; that person must die. He emphasizes that God created man in God`s image and that life is precious and murder is a terrible sin.

Genesis 9: 9 Then God blessed Noah and his sons and said to them, "Be fruitful and multiply and fill the earth. 2 Every beast of the earth and every bird of the sky and all that moves on the earth and all the fish of the sea will fear you and be terrified of you. They are given into your hand. 3 Every moving thing that lives will be food for you. I give you everything, just as I gave you the green plant.
4 "Only you shall not eat flesh with its life, that is, its blood. 5 But for your own lifeblood I will surely require a reckoning; from every animal will I require it; of man, too, will I require a reckoning for human life, of every man for that of his fellow man.
6 Whoever sheds the blood of man,
by man shall his blood be shed;
for God made man
in His own image.
7 And as for you, be fruitful and multiply; increase abundantly in the earth and multiply in it."

God also promises never to destroy all the life on earth again. He makes that covenant with Noah and his family and with all of the animals.

Genesis 9: 9 "As for Me, I establish My covenant with you, and with your descendants after you; 10 and with every living creature that is with you, the birds, the livestock, and every beast of the earth with you; of all that comes out of the ark, every beast of the earth. 11 I establish My covenant with you. Never again shall all flesh be cut off by the waters of a flood. Never again shall there be a flood to destroy the earth."
Absalom's murder of Ammon brings division to King David's family and

eventually of Israel itself.

2 Samuel 13: 26 Absalom said, "If not, allow my brother Amnon to go with us."
But the king replied to him, "Why should he go with you?" 27 But Absalom urged him until he sent Amnon and all of the king's sons along with him.
28 Now, Absalom had commanded his servant, "Look for Amnon to become carefree on account of the wine. Then I will say to you, 'Strike Amnon, and kill him.' Do not be afraid, for am not I myself commanding you? Be strong and brave." 29 So, the servants of Absalom did to Amnon that which Absalom had commanded. Then the sons of the king arose, each mounting his mule, and fled.

John the Baptist who announced the coming of the Messiah, who lived a holy life set apart from others preaching and reaching thousands of people for repentance, was given revelation that Jesus Christ is the Messiah. He saw him and pointed to him out to his disciples.

John 1: 35 Again, the next day John was standing with two of his disciples.
36 Looking upon Jesus as He walked, he said, "Look, the Lamb of God!"
Finally, a murder that was treachery as it was a friend who betrayed him to those who hated him.

Jesus Christ

Jesus Christ lived a holy life. He never sinned. He kept all the Levitical laws, never having to offer sacrifice because he never sinned. Jesus who preached the kingdom of God had come, is the same Jesus who manifested his message with miracles, signs and wonders. For three years, he preached the gospel of God desiring to commune with man. He healed the sick; he raised the dead. He feed the hungry with a miracle of provision. He was hated by many of the religious authorities who were jealous of his popularity with the people. Jesus reached thousands of people because of his simple but excellent way of teaching through parables. He made the Word of God, all the Levitical laws, understandable to ordinary people.

Acts 10: 36 The word which He sent to the children of Israel, preaching peace through Jesus Christ, who is Lord of all, 37 the word, which you know, that was proclaimed throughout all Judea, beginning from Galilee after the baptism which John preached: 38 how God anointed Jesus of Nazareth with the Holy Spirit and with power, who went about doing good and healing all who were oppressed by the devil, for God was with Him.
The Jewish authorities condemned Jesus to death because he proclaimed to

be one with God. Even though they expected the Messiah to come, they did not believe that Jesus was the Messiah because they were too religious to examine the proofs of Messiah that Jesus fulfilled. Some believed but they did it secretly because the majority was against Jesus. Jesus was arrested because one of his followers, Judas betrayed him and led the guards to Jesus so they could arrest him. He was taken to the high Jewish council – the Sanhedrin to be judged.

Although some of the people in that counsel had never personally heard Jesus preach of teach or do miracles, they found him guilty of blasphemy.

Mark 14: 60 Then the high priest stood up in the midst and asked Jesus, "Do You answer nothing? What is it which these men testify against You?"
61 But He kept silent and answered nothing.
Again the high priest asked Him, "Are You the Christ, the Son of the Blessed One?"
62 Jesus said, "I am. And you will see the Son of Man sitting at the right hand of Power and coming with the clouds of heaven."
63 The high priest tore his robes, saying, "What need do we have of any further witnesses? 64 You have heard the blasphemy. What do you think?"
The high priest torn his robes as a sign of horror and death. It meant that Jesus was guilty of death. The Jews ruled by Rome could not carry out a death sentence without Rome so they handed over one of their own Israelites to be charged and killed.

Pontius Piolet the Roman governor

The most powerful man in the region was Pontius Piolet. He could determine life or death and command Roman troops in the region. After meeting Jesus and questioning him, he had Jesus whipped and beaten. He once more questioned him. Piolet did not believe Jesus was guilty of anything and gave the people a chance to save him or a different person sentenced to death. The people chose Barabbas the criminal.

John 19: 4 Again Pilate went out and said to them, "Look, I am bringing Him out to you, that you may know that I find no guilt in Him." 5 Then Jesus came out, wearing the crown of thorns and the purple robe. Pilate said to them, "Here is the Man!"
6 When the chief priests and officers saw Him, they cried out, "Crucify Him! Crucify Him!"
Pilate said to them, "Take Him yourselves and crucify Him, for I find no guilt in Him."

Jesus was sentenced to death by crucifixion.
John 19: So they took Jesus and led Him away. 17 He went out, carrying His own cross, to a place called The Place of a Skull, which in Hebrew is called Golgotha. 18 There they crucified Him, and two others with Him, one on either side, and Jesus in the middle.
19 Pilate wrote a title and put it on the cross. The writing was:
JESUS OF NAZARETH, THE KING OF THE JEWS.

The Pharisees were outraged at the sign but Piolet kept it over Jesus. Ironically, what was meant to be an insult to the Jews, was prophetic.
Although on one level, Jesus death can be viewed as betrayal, capture, beating and murder, Jesus prophesied about himself before it occurred saying that he was giving his life.

John 10: 18 No one takes it from Me, but I lay it down Myself. I have power to lay it down, and I have power to take it up again. I received this command from My Father."

Mark 9: 31 For He was teaching His disciples, saying, "The Son of Man will be delivered into the hands of men, and they will kill Him. After He is killed, He will rise the third day." 32 But they did not understand the teaching and were afraid to ask Him.

Jesus knew he would die. He offered his life as a sacrifice. He died and the third day, he arose. Mary Magdalene was the first person to see him risen from the dead. She didn't recognize him at first until he revealed himself to her by saying her name.

John 20: 11 But Mary stood outside at the tomb weeping. As she wept, she stooped down and looked into the tomb, 12 and she saw two angels in white sitting where the body of Jesus had lain, one at the head and one at the feet.
13 They said to her, "Woman, why are you weeping?"
She said to them, "Because they have taken away my Lord, and I do not know where they have put Him." 14 When she had said this, she turned around and saw Jesus standing, but she did not know that it was Jesus.
15 Jesus said to her, "Woman, why are you weeping? Whom are you seeking?"
Supposing Him to be the gardener, she said to Him, "Sir, if You have carried Him away, tell me where You have put Him, and I will take Him away."
16 Jesus said to her, "Mary."
She turned and said to Him, "Rabboni!" (which means Teacher).

17 Jesus said to her, "Stop holding on to Me, for I have not yet ascended to My Father. But go to My brothers and tell them, 'I am ascending to My Father and your Father, to My God and your God.' "

The purpose for Jesus death, burial resurrection and ascension was that he gave his holy life as an atonement or payment for all sins of all people. The only possible solution to the sin of Adam and Eve was the total obedience of Jesus Christ. He took upon himself all the sins of all humans so that whoever believes in him would be saved.

Romans 10: This is the word of faith that we preach: 9 that if you confess with your mouth Jesus is Lord, and believe in your heart that God has raised Him from the dead, you will be saved, 10 for with the heart one believes unto righteousness, and with the mouth confession is made unto salvation. 11 For the Scripture says, "Whoever believes in Him will not be ashamed."[e] 12 For there is no distinction between Jew and Greek, for the same Lord over all is generous toward all who call upon Him. 13 For, "Everyone who calls on the name of the Lord shall be saved."[f]

Animal sacrifice doesn't have to be given anymore. Jesus blood shed for us not only covers our sins but erases them wholly. If we believe in Jesus we can live a life of holiness on earth.

1 John 1: 9 If we confess our sins, He is faithful and just to forgive us our sins and cleanse us from all unrighteousness.

We must sincerely receive Jesus as our Saviour. He paid the price of our sin with his own life. We can never repay such a gift, but we can honour God by receiving the gift of eternal life and the blessings that come with it. All of the blessings that God promised through all of His covenants with Israel are ours by faith in Jesus Christ. We can live in the blessings of chosen people by God by accepting Jesus as Saviour.

Galatians 3: 13 Christ has redeemed us from the curse of the law by being made a curse for us—as it is written, "Cursed is everyone who hangs on a tree"[f]— 14 so that the blessing of Abraham might come on the Gentiles through Jesus Christ, that we might receive the promise of the Spirit through faith.

Because of Jesus, we can commune with God. Jesus made a way for us to be the friends of God. Jesus made the way for us to talk with God and learn of Him and receive the Holy Spirit living within our very souls.

Romans 5: 5 Therefore, since we have been justified by faith, we have peace with God through our Lord Jesus Christ, 2 through whom we also have access by faith into this grace in which we stand, and so we rejoice in hope of the glory of God.

Jude 1: 24 Now to Him who is able to keep you from falling and to present you blameless before the presence of His glory with rejoicing, 2
Possibility of living in Spirit – life without sin – captain of our salvation
Jesus death, burial and resurrection brings hope to all people.

The sin of murder is horrible. Although a murderer will certainly be punished by the laws of our land, Jesus can cleanse the person from his sin and give that person peace with God.

7 CHAPTER

7th commandment

Deuteronomy 5: 18 You shall not commit adultery.

Adultery is any sex outside of marriage. That is a tough statement for many people to accept but that is what the scripture teaches.

Jesus teaching on divorce

Jesus was questioned by those trying to make exceptions for their divorce, but through it he not only comments on divorce but on marriage itself. The woman and the man are united in marriage. The two lives become one. Rather than living independent lives, they join to become one family.

Mark 10: 5 Jesus answered them, "Due to the hardness of your heart he wrote you this precept. 6 But from the beginning of the creation, God 'made them male and female.'[a] 7 'For this cause shall a man leave his father and mother, and cleave to his wife, 8 and the two shall be one flesh.'[b] So then they are no longer two, but one flesh. 9 What therefore God has joined together, let not man put asunder."
10 In the house His disciples asked Him concerning this matter again. 11 He said to them, "Whoever divorces his wife and marries another commits adultery against her. 12 And if a woman divorces her husband and marries another, she commits adultery."

There were some hard-hearted people who had many wives and would divorce a wife if for any reason she did not please him. Economically the woman got nothing. This was the way it was for thousands of years with men of wealth able to have wives and mistresses etc. There are still some civilizations that continue is polygamy. Such a culture oppresses women and girls. Jesus describes marriage in terms of monogamy. Jesus describes marriage as a covenant with God that throughout a lifetime the couple will be joined and committed to each other.

He is particularly harsh to the ones who questioned him trying to make excuses for their abuse of their wives and mistresses because he knows their hearts. They are trying to use his words with liberality so they can divorce freely. What it meant is they were free from all responsibility for those women. In that day (and still today in some places) a man could say out loud " I divorce you. I divorce you. I divorce you." And the woman would have to go try to earn a living or return to her parents without money or education or anything.

If you have been through a divorce, please do not believe there is no hope for you. Get right with God first. If you had a part in causing the divorce, repent. If you are a victim of divorce, take hope in God. God can heal you. I have had family members and close friends go through divorce. It is a horrible thing, particularly if there are children involved. He really impacts the lives of the children. It really impacts your life. If you are a Christian and you never believed it could happen but it did, please turn to God more than you veer have in the past. I have seen God heal people in the innermost being where your guts are ripped out of you. Often the person requires healing in the soul and in the spirit.

Sometimes the person decides to live single. God can redirect a person so that person can serve Him in a different capacity. I've known people who have continued teaching and preaching in spite of divorce because they will not let the devil stop their ministry as well as their marriage. I do not believe God's choice is ever divorce. The founding pastor of a church I attended used to call people into her office who were considering divorce. She flowed mightily in the gifts of the Spirit – especially the prophetic: she would get a word of wisdom or a word of knowledge about the situation and either one or both of the people would repent and recommit their lives to God and to each other. As part of minister's training, I took a mandatory marriage class; in that class, the teachers announced that if anyone had strife in their home or were even thinking about separation to phone them and that they would come and pray with them and see the marriage restored. They had a special gifting in that area and they were used by God to save marriages.

I have known of people who forgive the person for adultery and stay in the marriage. It is really tough to see but the rewards if the people commit to each other, are beyond what any person can imagine. It also saves their children from believing they have to choose sides. I have known of people who believe they will never rebound after a divorce. It is like a death to them and rather than realize that God has life for him or her, he or she believes he or she has no purpose. It is a lie of the devil to try to ruin the person's life. God will never let you live if there isn't a reason to live. You were created with a purpose. There is hope for you to be healed and fulfilled and possibly to remarry.

John 10: 10 The thief does not come, except to steal and kill and destroy. I came that they may have life, and that they may have it more abundantly.

King David

Adultery doesn't start in the bedroom. Adultery or unfaithfulness to your spouse starts by a breaking down of the hedge of protection that God puts around you. As a spider weaves together an intricate web to catch its prey, so does the devil attack a marriage. If the two married are not Christians, really I don't know how to explain why they stay together unless it is sheer will power and of course love.

There could be miscommunications between the partners in the marriage. Some vulnerable part of the other partner is exposed to the devil. Often other women or men will find the person attractive sexually. Please know, it occurs every day. With a hedge of protection around you though, you don't get caught by the flirting or the temptation. The pattern of any sin is in the words Jesus described in the following passage.

1 John 2: 16 For all that is in the world—the lust of the flesh, the lust of the eyes, and the pride of life—is not of the Father, but is of the world.

The lust of the eyes – what we see directly affects us. If we are watching half naked people, we are going to lust because God made the human body beautiful. You should turn your eyes away or not even watch such entertainment. The pride of life is very dangerous. It is the sin that Satan is the originator of as pride rose up in Lucifer so that he did not want to give God all the glory or the praise. He wanted to be as God. He was beautiful. He was a covering angel over God's throne, but at some instance he wanted to overthrow God and tried to do it.

Ezekiel 28: 13 You were in Eden,
the garden of God;
every precious stone was your covering:
the sardius, topaz, and the diamond,
the beryl, the onyx, and the jasper,
the sapphire, the emerald, and the carbuncle, and gold.
The workmanship of your settings and sockets was in you;
on the day that you were created, they were prepared.
14 You were the anointed cherub that covers,
and I set you there;
you were upon the holy mountain of God;
you walked up and down in the midst of the stones of fire.

15 You were perfect in your ways
from the day that you were created,
until iniquity was found in you.
16 By the multitude of your merchandise,
you were filled with violence in your midst,
and you sinned;
therefore I have cast you as profane out of the mountain of God;
and I have destroyed you, O covering cherub,
from the midst of the stones of fire.
17 Your heart was lifted up
because of your beauty;
you have corrupted your wisdom
by reason of your brightness;
I cast you to the ground,

Satan was thrown out of heaven. He lost his place. He is sentenced to eternal damnation. One third of the angels gathered with him. They too are in the realms of the earth. They hate man because God loves us. They would destroy us in any way they can. Usually pride affects a person when he or she is doing well. God prospers his servants. God provides more than enough and the person may become very wealthy. The person may develop much success and become famous. Often the person loses the truth – that God gave him or her everything including the gifts and talents to prosper. It is so important to keep the word of God in your eyes and ears and life so that you will remember that God is the almighty God and it is of His mercy that we are blessed. He delights in giving us the desires of our hearts.

It is God's desire to prosper his people. He will promote and give favour to His people. We must remain thankful to God as our source and also keep a humble heart about giving.

1 Timothy 6: 10 For the love of money is the root of all evil. While coveting after money, some have strayed from the faith and pierced themselves through with many sorrows.

The reason that God blesses you financially is so that you will have more than enough so you can give. Your life affects many types of people. As a family, you affect your neighbourhood; you affect your sphere of influence in the workplace and in the school system etc. all these places of your life you have a chance to make a difference. There may be television preachers or ministries that have blessed you by teaching you things you know have changed your life. Give of tithes, A person who regularly gives knowing that God has provided the seed or the finances, usually keeps using money to bless people. The more finances you receive, the more you can give: offerings and alms makes a difference helping those who might never receive help any other way. Keep thanking God for what you receive and keep giving to avoid the love of money.

Deuteronomy 8: 18 But you must remember the Lord your God, for it is He who gives you the ability to get wealth, so that He may establish His covenant which He swore to your fathers, as it is today.

King David

King David is known as a follower of God. He was anointed to be king, faithful to Saul even when Saul didn't deserve it. David never killed Saul although he had opportunity and Saul was hunting him and trying to kill David because of jealousy. David desired to bring God glory. One day though, things changed, It was David who was drawn away by his own lust and committed sin after sin trying to cover it up.

2 Samuel 11: 2 One evening when David arose from his bed and was walking on the roof of the king's house, from the roof he saw a woman bathing; and the woman was very beautiful. 3 So, David sent someone to inquire about the woman. And it was asked, "Is this not Bathsheba the daughter of Eliam, the wife of Uriah the Hittite?" 4 So David sent messengers, and took her; and she came to him, and he lay with her. When she had purified herself from her uncleanness, she returned to her house. 5 The woman conceived. So she sent a message and reported to David, "I am pregnant."

David noticed the beautiful naked woman bathing on her roof. He should have gone inside his home and prayed that he would not sin. Rather he stayed and enjoyed watching her. He lusted after her. He could have had any woman he wanted, but this woman was married. The king had the right to have sex with anyone in his kingdom. They were his servants. He gets Bathsheba. She becomes pregnant. Rather than confess this sin, he tries to cover over the sin. Her husband was away at war fighting for Israel. David brings him home and dines with him and gets him very drunk hoping he will go home to his wife and lie with her. He does not. He stays at the gates of the palace. He believes that his comrades are dying on the battlefield and he cannot take pleasure while they are risking their lives.

David writes a letter to the commander and has Uriah, Bathsheba's husband, deliver it. Within the letter is an order for the commander to send Uriah into the fiercest part of battle that he may not live. Faithful Uriah delivers his own death sentence. Afterwards, David takes Bathsheba as a wife. Their child dies as a result of the sin. David sinned by lusting after and taking Bathsheba. If he had repented God, perhaps things would not have been so terrible for him. He commits murder by his authority as King to eliminate the husband of a woman he loves. Abusing authority in this way grieves God. God sent the Prophet Nathan to David who revealed a judgement on him for taking Uriah's wife and murdering Uriah. God knows the things we do in secret. Judgement is given by God through the prophet.

2 Samuel 12: 7 Then Nathan told David, "You are this man! Thus says the
Lord, the God of Israel: I anointed you as king over Israel and I rescued
you from the hand of Saul. 8 I gave to you your master's house and your
master's wives into your arms, and I gave to you the house of Israel and
Judah. If this were too little, I would have continued to do for you much
more. 9 Why have you despised the word of the Lord by doing evil in His
sight? You struck down Uriah the Hittite with the sword, and you took his
wife as a wife for yourself. You killed him with the sword of the
Ammonites. 10 Now the sword will never depart from your house, because
you have despised Me and have taken the wife of Uriah the Hittite to be
your wife.
11 "Thus says the Lord: See, I will raise up trouble against you from within
your own house. I will take your wives before your eyes and will give them
to your neighbor, and he will lie with your wives in broad daylight. 12
Although you did it secretly, I will do this thing before all of Israel, and
under the sun."
13 Then David said to Nathan, "I have sinned against the Lord."

Because David repents truly for his horrible sins, God is merciful to him. Although the judgement is on his family because of what he has done, God lets him live until Solomon becomes King.

Adultery is a sin not only against you, but against your spouse and against God. The only hope for a person who commits adultery is to repent. God will forgive you. Repent to your spouse; he or she may forgive you. It is possible to recover from such a thing because of Jesus Christ.

8 CHAPTER NAME

8th Commandment

Deuteronomy 5: 19 You shall not steal.

Isaac is about to die and desires to give a blessing prayer to Esau. He tells him to go hunting.

Genesis 27: 2 He said, "I am old. I do not know the day of my death. 3 Therefore, please take your weapons, your quiver and your bow, and go out to the field and hunt game for me. 4 And prepare for me savory food, such as I love, and bring it to me that I may eat, so that my soul may bless you before I die."

Rebekah overhears the conversation and desires for Jacob to steal the blessing of Esau. She creates a plot to trick Isaac into blessing Jacob. She gives instruction to Jacob.

Genesis 27: 8 Now therefore, my son, listen to me as I command you. 9 Go now to the flock, and get me two choice young goats, so that I may prepare from them savory food for your father, such as he loves. 10 Then you will take it to your father, so that he may eat and so that he may bless you before his death."

Jacob has the correct first response. He realizes it is wrong. Rebekah condemns herself by saying that the curse be upon her. Jacob obeys his mother.

Genesis 27: 13 His mother said to him, "Let your curse be upon me, my son. Only listen to me and go get them for me."

Rebekah also prepares the food to assist in the plot.

Genesis 27: 14 He went and got them and brought them to his mother. Then his mother prepared savory food such as his father loved. 15 Then Rebekah took the best clothes belonging to her older son Esau, which were with her in the house, and put them on Jacob her younger son. 16 Then she put the skins of the young goats on his hands and on the smooth part of his neck. 17 She put the savory food and the bread, which she had prepared,

into the hands of her son Jacob.
Jacob lies and says he is Esau. Animal skins are on his arms and neck so dying Isaac feel him and believes it is Esau. Isaac gives his best blessing to Jacob believing it is Esau.
Genesis 27: 27 He came near and kissed him; and he smelled the smell of his clothing and blessed him and said,
"See, the smell of my son
is like the smell of the field
which the Lord has blessed.
28 Therefore, may God give you of the dew of heaven
and the fatness of the earth,
and plenty of grain and new wine.
29 Let peoples serve you,
and nations bow down to you.
Be master over your brothers,
and let your mother's sons bow down to you.
Cursed be everyone who curses you,
and blessed be those who bless you!"
Soon afterward, Esau comes with the food he caught and prepared. Isaac realizes he was deceived by Jacob and is overcome with emotion. Not only did Jacob trick him out of his birth right but he also stole his blessing. His desperate cry for a blessing moves Isaac with compassion but the blessing he receives is nothing like the tremendous blessing he prayed over Jacob.
Genesis 27: 34 When Esau heard the words of his father, he cried with a great and exceedingly bitter cry, and said to his father, "Bless me, even me also, O my father!"
35 He said, "Your brother came deceitfully and has taken away your blessing."

This deception is a deliberate plan and execution of stealing someone's blessing. The amazing thing is that although it was taken by deceit, God honours the blessing on Jacob. Eventually the two are restored in relationship.

Jacob escapes for his life because Esau is so angry with him, he might have killed him. Jacob goes to his uncle Laban to stay and immediately loves his daughter Rachel. Jacob agrees to work for his uncle for 7 years to marry Rachel. All those years of toil seemed as days because he anticipated his marriage to Rachel. Laban is more of a deceiver than Jacob was. It is possible that he knew he wanted to keep his nephew longer and so he deceived him.

Genesis 29: 16 Now Laban had two daughters. The name of the older was Leah, and the name of the younger was Rachel. 17 Leah's eyes were tender, but Rachel was beautiful in form and appearance. 18 Jacob loved Rachel, so he said, "I will serve you seven years for Rachel your younger daughter." 19 Laban said, "It is better that I give her to you than that I should give her to another man. Stay with me." 20 So Jacob served seven years for Rachel, and they seemed to him but a few days because of the love he had for her. There is a wedding feast. Jacob believes he has married Rachel.
Genesis 29: 22 Laban gathered together all the men of the place and prepared a feast. 23 But in the evening he took Leah his daughter and brought her to Jacob, and Jacob had relations with her. 24 Laban gave Zilpah his maid to his daughter Leah for a maidservant.
25 In the morning Jacob discovered it was Leah, and he said to Laban, "What is this you have done to me? Did I not serve you for Rachel? Why then have you tricked me?"

Jacob knows what it is like to be tricked out of his blessing. He desired to marry Rachel but her sister Leah was given instead. Laban responds as a shrewd businessman who bargains for 7 more years of service to marry Rachel. Jacob still loves Rachel and does work the extra 7 years. Now he has to care for both of the wives. He has relations with both and children but he did not love Leah the way he loved Rachel.

Genesis 29: 26 Then Laban said, "It is not the custom in our country to marry off the younger before the firstborn. 27 Fulfill the period of seven days for this one, and we will give you the other also in return for serving me another seven years."

After the other 7 years, Jacob desires to return to his home with his wives and children. Laban is chasing him. Jacob fears that perhaps Laban won't let him keep his wives and children. Laban accuses him of stealing his idol god. Jacob knows he did not take it and utters a curse believing it is trick of Laban.

Genesis 29: 31 Then Jacob answered and said to Laban, "Because I was afraid, for I thought that you would take your daughters from me by force. 32 But anyone with whom you find your gods, let him not live. In the presence of our kinsmen, point out what I have that is yours and take it." For Jacob did not know that Rachel had stolen them.

Rachel sits on the idol to hide it and pretends she has her monthly period so that no one will search her because women were considered unclean while they were menstruating. She not only steals, she steals an idol god. She lies pretending she has not taken it.

The lying and stealing amongst the family was like a soap opera. The result though is that Laban and Jacob make a covenant peace pact an both promise to live rightly by each other.

Achan

Joshua is leading Israel into the promised land. God has given them victory over Jericho. God's instructions were to take nothing from these people because they were idol worshippers. At the battle of Ai (Joshua 7) There is a terrible defeat of Israel. Jesus cannot understand it. He tears his garments and cries out to god for mercy because he believed all the people had obeyed God. God speaks to him frankly that someone has sinned.

Joshua 7: 10 Then the Lord said to Joshua, "Stand up! Why have you fallen on your face? 11 Israel has sinned, and they have broken My covenant that I commanded them. They took from the things dedicated for destruction. They have stolen, acted deceitfully, and put them among their own possessions. 12 Therefore the children of Israel cannot stand before their enemies. They turn their backs to their enemies because they have become dedicated for destruction. I will not be with you anymore if you do not destroy the things dedicated for destruction in your midst.

Joshua 7: 13 "Get up! Consecrate the people and say, 'Consecrate yourselves for tomorrow, for thus says the Lord, the God of Israel: "Things dedicated for destruction are in your midst, O Israel. You are not able to stand before your enemies until you remove the things dedicated for destruction from your midst."

God's words are harsh. If even one person disobeys, God's presence will not be with them for victory. They cast lots (draw straws) and the sin is pinpointed to Achan's family.

Joshua 7: 19 Then Joshua said to Achan, "O my son, give glory to the Lord, the God of Israel, and give Him praise! Tell me what you have done! Do not hold back anything from me."

Joshua 7: 20 Achan answered Joshua and said, "Indeed, I sinned against the Lord, the God of Israel. This is what I did: 21 When I saw among the plundered goods a beautiful robe from Babylon, two hundred shekels of silver,[a] and a gold bar weighing fifty shekels,[b] I coveted them, so I took them. They are hidden in the ground in my tent. The silver is underneath them."

Achan stole from the idol worshippers because he coveted the things. He took them and brings disaster on all of Israel. Joshua and Israel stone Achan and his family for their sin against God.

The importance of this incident is that even though there were thousands of people in the battle, even though almost everyone obeyed, God knows the secret things. God pointed to the one who sinned because He would tolerate no disobedience. It is an example to all of Israel that God sees all things and knows all things and that total obedience was a requirement. It also causes them to rely on God for directions about battles rather than simply going by their own plans.

After God give Moses the tablets with the commandments on them, He also gives other laws and commandments (total 613) so that Israel will have rules to live by that would be pleasing to God. Keeping these rules, was a guideline for life in the promised land. The people had no country for over 400 years so these laws were the heritage for Israel. Many of them were used by North American countries when the countries began.

Restitution

Restitution or repayment or justice of what was stolen is made clear by God. In almost all cases, if anyone stole something, it was to be replaced of equal value.

Exodus 22: 1If a man steals an ox or a sheep and kills it or sells it, then he shall repay five oxen for an ox, and four sheep for a sheep.
2 If a thief is caught breaking in and is struck so that he dies, then there will be no blood guilt for him. 3 If the sun has risen on him, then there is blood guilt for him.
4 He must make full restitution. If he has nothing, then he will be sold for his theft. 4 If the stolen item is in fact found alive in his possession, whether it be an ox, or donkey, or sheep, then he shall repay double.
5 If a man causes a field or vineyard to be eaten and puts out his beast so that it feeds in another man's field, he must make restitution of the best of his own field and of the best of his own vineyard.
Salomon had revelation from God about stealing of a person who is starving and takes food. The payment is much steeper but the thief is given mercy because in truth Israel should be caring for the poor among them by giving of alms.

Proverbs 6: 30 Men do not despise a thief if he steals
to satisfy himself when he is hungry.
31 But if he is found, he will restore sevenfold;
he will give all the substance of his house.

Satan

Jesus compares himself as a good shepherd while he describes the devil as one who comes to rob, kill, destroy.

John 10: 10 The thief does not come, except to steal and kill and destroy. I came that they may have life, and that they may have it more abundantly.

He is clearly speaking of the devil. Because Satan sinned against God and is awaiting his eternal judgement in the realms of the earth, he hates man. He hates us because we are God's people, made in the likeness of God. We were created in God's image. The devil's future is certain – it is eternal damnation. Humans have free will to choose God or not to choose God. The devil would try to influence people to steal from them the hope of heaven. Often it has to do with sin and bondage and stealing people's lives from them by making them addicted to things.

If the devil could, he would kill you. He cannot do it, though, if you are serving God. God places a hedge of protection around you that shields you from such things. Some people blames God for disasters. God does not bring disasters on people. Outside of God's will there is the curse of Adam with all types of curses and negative things. Living in covenant with God, Christians are protected from these things. Destruction is the opposite of God. God created all things for His glory. God gave man the ability to create and design and express gifts and design things that will help others. Destruction is not from God but the result of the sin of Adam.

Jesus makes this comparison so that people will know that if they choose him, they will be blessed and have abundant life. He also lets them know that if they choose the devil, they will be at the peril of their lives and their souls.

Jesus has a traitor amongst his group of 12 disciples. Judas who was the treasurer was stealing from the ministry funds. Judas saw Mary of Bethany pour expensive perfume over Jesus feet. Judas believed it was a waste of money because he didn't know the treasure of the Messiah in his midst. Mary poured all the best she had for him and Jesus said she had done it as unto his burial.

John 12: 4 But one of His disciples, Judas Iscariot, Simon's son, who would betray Him, said, 5 "Why was this ointment not sold for three hundred denarii[b] and given to the poor?" 6 He said this, not because he cared for the poor, but because he was a thief. And having the money box, he used to steal what was put in it.

The Apostle Paul

The Apostle Paul was preaching mostly to the Gentiles or people who didn't know the one true God, many of them were idol worshippers. He gave instructions about important matters in the books of the Bible that he wrote. He made it clear that no one should steal and he gave the solution to someone who is a thief – start giving.

Ephesians 4: 28 Let him who steals steal no more. Instead, let him labor, working with his hands things which are good, that he may have something to share with him who is in need.

The opposite of stealing is giving. If the person who steals repents, the next thing he or she should do is start giving. Giving is being like God. God gives us all things to enjoy.

1 Timothy 6: 17 Command those who are rich in this world that they not be conceited, nor trust in uncertain riches, but in the living God, who richly gives us all things to enjoy.

2 Peter 1: 3 His divine power has given to us all things that pertain to life and godliness through the knowledge of Him who has called us by His own glory and excellence,

9 CHAPTER

9th commandment

LYING

Deuteronomy 5: 20 You shall not bear false witness against your neighbor. False witness or lying is a sin. The first meaning of false witness was used because if someone were to be convicted of a crime, 2 or 3 witnesses had to agree that they witnessed it. One person alone was not enough. To falsely say would be committing a terrible sin because an innocent person may be sentenced or a guilty person could go free.

The first lie originated in the Garden of Eden. Satan uttered the first lie. It was misquoting God or using similar words but not the words that God had said. God had instructed Adam (and Eve) not to eat of the fruit of the Tree of the Knowledge of Good and Evil or they would surely die. Satan possessed the serpent and used part of God's words and partly a lie. God did say they could have the fruit of any other tree – just not the Tree of the Knowledge of Good and Evil.

Genesis 3: 1 Now the serpent was more subtle than any beast of the field which the Lord God had made. And he said to the woman, "Has God said, 'You shall not eat of any tree of the garden'?"

Eve's response should have been the truth; Eve herself lied in her response to the serpent. She added in extra words that God did not say such as you should not even touch it [the tree of knowledge of good and evil].

Genesis 3: 2 And the woman said to the serpent, "We may eat of the fruit from the trees of the garden; 3 but from the fruit of the tree which is in the midst of the garden, God has said, 'You will not eat of it, nor will you touch it, or else you will die.' "

Satan speaks through the serpent another lie which contradicts totally the words God spoke to them. The serpent says that they surely will not die. That is a direct lie. Also, he adds in a lie to seduce the woman into sinning. He says they will become as gods and have wisdom beyond what they have known to know good and evil.

Genesis 3: 4 Then the serpent said to the woman, "You surely will not die! 5 For God knows that on the day you eat of it your eyes will be opened and you will be like God, knowing good and evil."

The lies form a web or snare to Eve. She sees the fruit. No longer does she see it the same. Previously she saw the fruit as forbidden. Now she sees the tree was good for food. The lies have created a false sense in her that ignites lust in her for the forbidden. She no longer remembers God's words. She sees the fruit on the tree as desirable to make her wise. Her senses are lusting after what God has forbidden. She takes of the fruit believing all the lies the serpent has spun.

The immediate response is sin nature. They have disobeyed God. Adam and Eve no longer see each other as pure. They realize they are naked. They try to hide their shame by using leaves to cover themselves. They try to hide from God. They did not immediately die physically but their communion with God has died. They are no longer spiritually pure.

Genesis 3: 6 When the woman saw that the tree was good for food, that it was pleasing to the eyes and a tree desirable to make one wise, she took of its fruit and ate; and she gave to her husband with her, and he ate. 7 Then the eyes of both were opened, and they knew that they were naked. So they sewed fig leaves together and made coverings for themselves.

Abraham

Abraham is known for his faith and his waiting for his promises to come to pass, but he is a liar and he does it to protect his own life. Somehow God blesses him anyone. He travels to Egypt with his wife and all his people and cattle etc. He fears that the king will want his wife and might kill him for it, so he lies and says she is my sister. The truth is they are related but the way he announces it is as if she were a single free woman available.

God is merciful to the king because he warns him in a dream not to lie with Sarai because she is married; if he does it, he will surely die.

Genesis 20: 6 2 Then Abraham said about Sarah his wife, "She is my sister." So Abimelek, king of Gerar, sent for her and took Sarah.
3 But God came to Abimelek in a dream by night and said to him, "You are a dead man because of the woman whom you have taken, for she is a man's wife."
4 Abimelek had not gone near her, and he said, "Lord, will You slay a

righteous nation? 5 Did he not say to me, 'She is my sister,' and did not even she herself say, 'He is my brother'? In the integrity of my heart and innocence of my hands I have done this."
6 And God said to him in a dream, "Yes, I know that you did this in the integrity of your heart. For I also kept you from sinning against Me. Therefore, I did not let you touch her. 7 Therefore return the man's wife, for he is a prophet and he will pray for you. Moreover, you will live. However, if you do not return her, know that you will surely die, you and all who are yours."

The king is so reverent of God's warning he gives Abraham many things and even a sum of money to prove that Sarah is innocent and that he has not defiled her. Abraham prays a blessing on them. Abraham's lie to protect himself rather than his wife is cowardly but God does bless him anyway.

Geneis 20: 17 So Abraham prayed to God, and God healed Abimelek, his wife, and his female servants. Then they bore children. 18 For the Lord had closed up all the wombs of the house of Abimelek because of Sarah, Abraham's wife.

Dinah loses her virginity

In Genesis 34 a terrible incidence of rape of Dinah, one of Leah's daughters is recorded. The man who raped her wants to marry her. In this instance of injustice towards the woman, she is not even consulted about it. Her family would make the decision.

Her brothers say they cannot give her to uncircumcised people because it is against their covenant with God. It is true certainly. God forbid his people from marrying idol worshippers or those who are not in covenant with God. They twist the truth of God's Covenant with them as though if the man was circumcised he would be acceptable. The truth was he was an idol worshipper and he raped her. He should not have been considered at all. They suggest that all the men of the family get circumcised. I'm not sure if they knew it would be accepted because not many grown men would voluntarily be circumcised because of the pain it causes but also because they did not know the God of the covenant or the meaning of being set apart for God.

Genesis 34: 13 The sons of Jacob answered Shechem and Hamor his father deceitfully, because he had defiled Dinah their sister. 14 They said to them, "We cannot do this. To give our sister to one who is uncircumcised would be a disgrace to us. 15 But we will consent to you in this: If you will become as we are, that is, every one of your males be circumcised, 16 then we will give our daughters to you, and we will take your daughters to us, and we will dwell with you, and we will become one people. 17 But if you will not listen to us and be circumcised, then we will take our daughter, and we will leave."

The men of Shechem agree to be circumcised. This is an huge concession for them to make because they do not know God at all. Jacob's sons use the covenant of Abraham to weaken the men so that they can kill them and destroy the town. They get revenge on the crime against their sister but it is not just. All of the town is destroyed. They use God's covenant as a lure to kill the men.

Genesis 34: 25 On the third day, when they were in pain, two of Jacob's sons, Simeon and Levi, Dinah's brothers, took their swords and went to the unsuspecting city and killed all the males. 26 They killed Hamor and Shechem his son with the edge of the sword and took Dinah out of the house of Shechem and departed. 27 The sons of Jacob came upon the slain and looted the city, because they had defiled their sister. 28 They took their flocks and their herds, their donkeys and whatever was in the city and in the fields. 29 They took captive and looted all their wealth, all their little ones, and their wives, even all that was in each house.

Joseph's brothers

Joseph who is Jacob's favourite son is gifted by God with dreams and shares them, not so wisely with his brothers. It seems as though he is always bragging. Also, he is a tattle tale on his brothers. His brothers are jealous of him and their anger against them causes them to take him by force. Their desire was to kill him. Judah speaks something that is less a crime but certainly still a horrible crime. He suggests they sell their brother as a slave.

Genesis 37 : 26 Then Judah said to his brothers, "What profit is it if we kill our brother and cover up his blood? 27 Come, let us sell him to the Ishmaelites, and let us not lay our hand on him, for he is our brother and our own flesh." So his brothers agreed.

28 Then when the Midianite merchants passed by, they drew Joseph up and lifted him out of the pit and sold Joseph to the Ishmaelites for twenty shekels of silver.[b] They took Joseph to Egypt.

29 When Reuben returned to the pit and saw that Joseph was not in the pit, he tore his clothes. 30 He returned to his brothers, and said, "The boy is not there, and I, where can I go?"

Joseph's brothers throw him in a pit. As they see the slave traders coming, they sell their brother to them. They plot together to create a lie to tell Jacob. Not only do they agree on the lie, they provide false evidence; they slay a goat and pour its blood over the multicolour jacket that Jacob made for Joseph. They lie pretending they don't know what could have happened to Joseph giving false evidence. It completely grieves Jacob and for years he believed his son died. This lie gives the brothers freedom from Joseph's bragging about his dreams. It gives them more freedom without Joseph watching them. It causes many years of hardship for Joseph. It is a miracle, but God uses Joseph and blesses him in spite of all these things.

Genesis 37: 31 They took Joseph's coat and killed a young goat and dipped the coat in the blood. 32 Then they took the coat of many colors and brought it to their father and said, "This we have found. Do you know whether it is your son's robe or not?"
33 He knew it and said, "It is my son's coat. A wild beast has devoured him. Joseph has without a doubt been torn into pieces."
34 Jacob tore his clothes and put sackcloth on his waist and mourned for his son many days. 35 All his sons and all his daughters rose up to comfort him, but he refused to be comforted. And he said, "For I will go down into the grave mourning for my son." So his father wept for him.

.

Joseph

Even though Joseph was sold into slavery, a terrible thing, his master could recognize much potential in him and gave him authority in his home. He was the manager of the home of Potiphar. God prospered Joseph even in his situation. It's important to show that it was Joseph who had God's blessing on him. He was not only Jacob's favourite but had a special anointing from God on him. Joseph was also handsome. His master's wife lusted after him. Joseph honoured God and his master. He would not lie with her, escaping her with her holding onto his clothing. He ran from the temptation to shame God or his master.

Genesis 39: Now Joseph was handsome and well-built. 7 After a time, his master's wife took notice of Joseph and said, "Lie with me."
8 But he refused and said to his master's wife, "My master does not concern himself with anything concerning me in the house, and he has committed all that he has to my charge. 9 There is none greater in this house than I. He has kept nothing back from me but you, because you are his wife. How then can I do this great wickedness and sin against God?" 10 She spoke to Joseph every day, but he did not listen to her about lying with her or being with her.

11 But it happened one day that Joseph went into the house to do his
work, and none of the men of the house was there. 12 She caught him by
his clothing, saying, "Lie with me." But he left his clothing in her hand and
fled and got outside.

Potiphar's wife is very angry. She has been rejected. She normally got anything she wanted. She was wealthy. She was important. She covered her own lust by her lies. She feared for her own life as if her husband found out what really happened, certainly she would be punished. She lies and blames Joseph for trying to rape her. She keeps his clothing as a witness against him. Once more clothing is used as false evidence.

Genesis 39: 13 When she saw that he had left his clothing in her hand and
had fled outside, 14 she called to the men of her house and spoke to them,
saying, "See, he has brought in a Hebrew among us to humiliate us. He
came in to me to lie with me, and I cried out with a loud voice. 15 When he
heard that I lifted up my voice and cried out, he left his clothing with me,
fled, and got outside."
16 She laid up his clothing next to her until his master came home. 17 She
spoke to him using these words, saying, "The Hebrew servant, whom you
have brought to us, came in to me to mock me. 18 When I lifted up my
voice and cried out, he left his clothing with me and fled outside."

Because of Potiphar's wife's lie, Joseph is put in the prison for a crime he did not commit. Even though God has mercy on him and blesses him, he still endures much hardship in the prison until God raises him up. He does get favour in the prison itself and is raised up to be a manger of the prison.

The Gabionites

There are people who lie to protect others or themselves. The Gibionites hear about the miracles God has done for Israel in delivering them from Egypt and giving them victory in every battle. They are fearful of Israel and the God of Israel so they plan and commit a schemed lie to protect themselves. They pretend to be from a distant land and they want to make a peace treaty with Israel. Joshua was instructed to kill all the inhabitants of the promised land because they were idol worshippers. The Gabionites pretend they are from outside the promised land. They pretend to have brought gifts of a peace treaty that have grown old because of their long journey. They bring old worn out things as evidence. Once more false evidence is used to support their lies.

Joshua 9: 1 But when the inhabitants of Gibeon heard what Joshua had done to Jericho and Ai, 4 they acted craftily, and took old sacks on their donkeys, and old wineskins, torn and mended, 5 old and patched sandals on their feet, and old garments on themselves. All the bread of their provision was dry and crumbly. 6 They went to Joshua at the Gilgal settlement and said to him and the children of Israel, "We have come from a distant land. Now make a pact with us."
7 Then the children of Israel said to these Hivites, "Perhaps you live among us, so how could we make a pact with you?"
8 Yet they said to Joshua, "We are your slaves."
Joshua said to them, "Who are you, and where do you come from?"
9 They said to him, "We, your slaves, have come from a very distant land because of the name of the Lord your God, for we heard news of Him and all He did in Egypt 10 and all that He did to the two Amorite kings on the other side of the Jordan, King Sihon of Heshbon and King Og of Bashan in Ashtaroth. 11 So our elders and all the inhabitants of our country said to us, 'Take food provisions for the journey and go to meet them. Say to them, "We are your slaves. So now, make a pact with us." ' 12 This bread of ours was hot as we took it from our homes on the day we left to come to you, but now, see, it is dry and crumbly. 13 These wineskins that we filled were new, but see, they are ripped open. These clothes and sandals wore out due to the very long journey."

Joshua did not consult God in it, but he should have. He saw the evidence provided by the Gibionites and believed it to be true. He was deceived into making a peace treaty with them. Within 3 days, the people of Israel realize they had been lied to and they have made a peace treaty with their enemy. They were bound by their swearing of the treaty to God.

Joshua 9: 16 Three days after they had made a covenant with them, they heard that they were neighbors to them and lived among them. 17 So the children of Israel set out and came to their cities on the third day. Their cities were Gibeon, Kephirah, Beeroth, and Kiriath Jearim. 18 Now the children of Israel did not attack them, for the leaders of the congregation had sworn an oath to them by the Lord, the God of Israel, so the congregation murmured against the leaders.
19 Yet all the leaders said to the whole congregation, "We swore to them by the Lord God of Israel, so now we may not harm them. 20 This is what we will do to them. We will let them live so that wrath will not come upon us due to the oath that we swore to them." 21 The leaders of the congregation also said to them, "Let them live!" So they became woodcutters and water carriers for the whole congregation, as the leaders told them.

Although they lied to protect themselves, Israel kept its oath with the Gibionites but assigned to them a position of service not an equal position but they were as servants of Israel, but their lives were spared.

Ahab

Ahab the king is known for much evil and is his wife Jezebel. The king had much land and much money and wielded his power throughout Israel. He desired the garden that belonged to Naboth. Naboth desired to keep it for sentimental reasons as it was his family inheritance. Because Ahab is used to getting his way always, he sulked about it. He shares his desire for the land with his evil wife Jezebel. She promises to get the vineyard.

1 Kings 21: 21 Now Naboth the Jezreelite had a vineyard in Jezreel right by the palace of Ahab king of Samaria. 2 And after this Ahab spoke to Naboth, saying, "Give me your vineyard, so that I can have it for a garden of herbs, because it is near to my house, and I will give you a better vineyard for it, or if you prefer, I will give you its worth in money."
3 Naboth said to Ahab, "The Lord forbid that I should give you the inheritance of my fathers."

Jezebel not only promises to get the land, she does things wicked to do it. First, she reminds the king he is powerful. She uses the king's authority to murder an innocent man. She spins a web to trap Naboth into certain and unjust death. She uses the guise to condemn him. She arranges for false witnesses to be paid to lie to condemn Naboth to death for cursing God and the king. She uses her husband's seal of authority to seal the command. It is done as she orders and Naboth is condemned to death. His vineyard is now the property of Ahab.

1 Kings 21: 7 Jezebel his wife said to him, "Are you not the governor of the kingdom of Israel? Get up and eat bread, and let your heart be happy, for I will get the vineyard of Naboth the Jezreelite for you."
8 So she wrote letters in Ahab's name and sealed them with his seal and sent the letters to the elders and to the nobles that were in the city where Naboth lived. 9 In the letters she wrote,
"Proclaim a fast, and set Naboth on high among the people, 10 and set two men, sons of Belial,[a] before him, to bear witness against him, saying, 'You blasphemed God and the king.' And then carry him out and stone him, so that he will die."

The Apostle Paul

Paul was winning souls among the Gentiles. He had to speak to them about the character of Christ because they had been living according to their soul and doing things that are fleshly because they did not know any other way. He instructs them on many things but I have emphasized the parts that he spoke about speaking the truth and not giving false witness. He explains that they must be renewed in the spirit. It is only through life in the spirit that they can overcome their fleshly passions and sins.

Ephesians 4: 15 But, speaking the truth in love, we may grow up in all things into Him, who is the head, Christ Himself, 16 from whom the whole body is joined together and connected by every joint and ligament, as every part effectively does its work and grows, building itself up in love.
25 Therefore, putting away lying, let every man speak truthfully with his neighbor, for we are members of one another.
20 But you did not learn about Christ in this manner, 21 if indeed you have heard Him and have been taught by Him, as the truth is in Jesus: 22 that you put off the former way of life in the old nature, which is corrupt according to the deceitful lusts, 23 and be renewed in the spirit of your mind; 24 and that you put on the new nature, which was created according to God in righteousness and true holiness.

Pharisees lying witnesses against Jesus

Not only did the Pharisees pay Judas for betraying Jesus to them, some of them gave false witness at his trial at the Sanhedrin. They accused him but no true evidence was given.

Matthew 26: 59 The chief priests and the elders and the entire Sanhedrin searched for false witness against Jesus to put Him to death, 60 but they found none. Yes, though many false witnesses came forward, they found none.

At last two false witnesses came forward 61 and said, "This fellow said, 'I am able to destroy the temple of God and to build it in three days.' "
The book of Revelation gives us a list of things that keep people out of the kingdom of God. The sins listed are pretty horrible because it includes sexual impurity, murder and sorcery. In the list Lying or bearing false witness is listed

Warning about lying
the sorcerers, the idolaters, and all liars shall have their portion in the lake which burns with fire and brimstone. This is the second death."

Lying is listed in sins that can keep a person from the kingdom of God. It shows God's hatred of sin. Lying is considered as serious as adultery or sorcery.

10 CHAPTER

10th commandment

Deuteronomy 5: 21 You shall not covet your neighbor's wife, nor shall you covet your neighbor's house, his field, his male servant, his female servant, his ox, his donkey, or anything that belongs to your neighbor.

Covet

To covet something is to desire it strongly. Desiring what belongs to someone else is the sin. It is not wrong to desire something, but to want what belongs to someone else is wrong. God is merciful; ask for your own. For example, you may see a sharp red Camaro car and think I like the car; I'd like to have one of those. That is not a sin. It's normal for humans to desire things. Things that are clearly set apart or owned by someone else are not your property and you have no right to them. Covetousness is a lusting for someone or something that is not yours.

In North America, we have freedoms to get jobs, create companies etc. It is possible for anyone to get an idea and become wealthy because of it. There are people who hate the rich or wealthy because they covet their wealth. People may say negative things about the person or the company because they desire the wealth of that person. This is a form of covetousness. That type of person believes it is easier for someone else to acquire wealth than it is for his or her. That person, if a Christian, should know that God delights in blessing his people.

Deuteronomy 8: 18 But you must remember the Lord your God, for it is He who gives you the ability to get wealth, so that He may establish His covenant which He swore to your fathers, as it is today.

God's covenant of blessing is on all people who believe in Him and who honour Him. That means should you set your heart on something (nothing illegal or immoral) it would be God's pleasure to bless you with it. God want to give you the desires of your heart. Pray, seek God, ask of Him and receive from Him the things He gives. If a person truly knows God, he or she knows that God is good and gives abundantly to his people.

Luke 12: 31 But seek the kingdom of God, and all these things shall be given to you.
32 "Do not be afraid, little flock, for it is your Father's good pleasure to give you the kingdom
Lucifer coveted God's glory

The first covetousness occurred with Lucifer when he sinned against God. He was the covering cherub over God's throne. He was kind of like a worship leader. He gave all glory and honour to God. He sinned because he wanted to keep the glory that goes to God. He coveted the praise and glory that he was receiving and giving to God. He wanted to overthrow God. It was rebellion. Because of his evil desire, possibly also his beauty and position, one third of the angels sided with Him. God immediately threw them out of heaven and into the atmosphere of the earth,

Ezekiel 28: 14 You were the anointed cherub that covers,
and I set you there;
you were upon the holy mountain of God;
you walked up and down in the midst of the stones of fire.
15 You were perfect in your ways
from the day that you were created,
until iniquity was found in you.
16 By the multitude of your merchandise,
you were filled with violence in your midst,
and you sinned;
therefore I have cast you as profane out of the mountain of God;
and I have destroyed you, O covering cherub,
from the midst of the stones of fire.
17 Your heart was lifted up
because of your beauty;
you have corrupted your wisdom
by reason of your brightness;
I cast you to the ground,
I lay you before kings, that they may see you.
18 You have defiled your sanctuaries
by the multitude of your iniquities, by the iniquity of your trade;

Cain coveted Abel's sacrifice and God's favour

Cain coveted Abel's offering to God. Cain coveted God's approval of his own offering. He wanted the approval of God but would not submit to God. God speaks with him revealing the true condition of his heart. He should do the right thing and he too would receive the blessing of God.

Cain grows angry and rebellious and ends up killing Abel rather than repent of the sin in his heart.

Genesis 4: 6 The Lord said to Cain, "Why are you angry? Why is your countenance fallen? 7 If you do well, shall you not be accepted?[a] But if you do not do well, sin is crouching at the door. It desires to dominate you, but you must rule over it."

Jacob coveted his brother's birthright and blessing

Jacob coveted Esau's birthright. His very name was "heel catcher" or deceiver. Jacob was his mother's favourite. He liked doing things around the home. Esau was a hunter and his dad's favourite. Jacob cooked something. Esau come desiring it. Jacob could have given him some and made a different deal. Jacob should have known God could bless him also, but Jacob believed he had to have Esau's birthright in order to have a good life. He bargained for his birthright. Esau esteemed such a treasure too lightly and traded it for a pot of stew, Jacob tricked his brother into giving up something that was considered precious. God promised to bless the first born in a special way.

Genesis 25: 29 Now Jacob cooked a stew; and Esau came in from the field and he was famished. 30 So Esau said to Jacob, "Please feed me some of that red stew, for I am famished." Therefore, his name was called Edom.
31 Then Jacob said, "First sell me your birthright."
32 Esau said, "Look, I am about to die; of what use is the birthright to me?"
33 Then Jacob said, "Swear to me this day." So he swore to him, and he sold his birthright to Jacob.
34 Then Jacob gave Esau bread and lentil stew. Then he ate and drank, arose, and went his way.
Thus Esau despised his birthright.
Later, Jacob coveted Esau's blessing.

Jacob covets

The blessing was the most important thing a parent could impart to his children. It was a special prayer passing on the blessings of Abraham. It was a way of honouring God and passing the truths of the covenant to the remaining children.

Although Rachel is the inspiration to steal the birthright, Jacob agrees and places animal skins on his hands and neck. He gets a goat to cook so

Jacob can give him the blessing instead of Esau. The blessing he steals includes all areas of life in agriculture, in blessings from heaven, finally ending with the exact words God spoke to Abraham in covenant.

Genesis 27: 27 He came near and kissed him; and he smelled the smell of his clothing and blessed him and said, "See, the smell of my son
is like the smell of the field
which the Lord has blessed.
28 Therefore, may God give you of the dew of heaven
and the fatness of the earth,
and plenty of grain and new wine.
29 Let peoples serve you,
and nations bow down to you.
Be master over your brothers,
and let your mother's sons bow down to you.
Cursed be everyone who curses you,
and blessed be those who bless you!"

Jacob receives the blessings of the covenant but not until he learns from his uncle Laban. God does prosper him; God transforms his heart so that he can receive with a right heart attitude honouring God for blessing him.

Ahab coveted the vineyard of Naboth

Ahab could have purchased any other plot of land. Ahab was wealthy and powerful; instead of seeking for a similar plot of land, he wanted the exact piece of land that Naboth owned. He wanted the exact vineyard that Naboth would not sell because it was his inheritance. The covetousness affected him so much, it affected his spirit. He lusted after what was not his. It affected his countence or presence. Jezabel, helps him to get what is not his by lying and saying he is the king of Israel so he could get anything he wanted. The truth was Ahab should have feared God. He let his wife get the plot of land for him by murdering an innocent man.

1 Kings 21: 3 Naboth said to Ahab, "The Lord forbid that I should give you the inheritance of my fathers."
4 Ahab returned home angry and depressed because of the answer Naboth the Jezreelite had given him, for he had said, "I will not give you the inheritance of my fathers." He lay down on his bed and sulked and would not eat any bread.
5 But Jezebel his wife came to him and said, "Why is your spirit so sad that you refuse to eat bread?"

6 And he said to her, "Because I spoke to Naboth the Jezreelite and said to him, 'Give me your vineyard for money; or else, if you prefer, I will give you another vineyard for it.' And he answered, 'I will not give you my vineyard.' "
7 Jezebel his wife said to him, "Are you not the governor of the kingdom of Israel? Get up and eat bread, and let your heart be happy, for I will get the vineyard of Naboth the Jezreelite for you."
After the murder of Naboth, Ahab goes to the vineyard to take possession. He desired it; it was finally his. The prophet Elijah goes to him because God saw the evil done to the innocent man Naboth. It is a severe word of doom that the prophet speaks over Ahab. He condemns Ahab for his part in murdering Naboth to take his land. He curses him that he would die in a field so that dogs would lick his blood. Ahab calls Elijah his enemy, while the truth is that Ahab is God's enemy.

1 Kings 21: 17 The word of the Lord came to Elijah the Tishbite, saying: 18
Arise, go down to meet Ahab, king of Israel, who is in Samaria. He is now
in the vineyard of Naboth, where he has gone down to possess it. 19 You
shall speak to him, saying, "Thus says the Lord: Have you killed and also taken possession?" And you shall speak to him, saying, "Thus says the Lord: In the place where dogs licked the blood of Naboth, dogs will lick your own blood!"
20 Ahab said to Elijah, "Have you found me, my enemy?"

The prophet Elijah condemns Ahab to lose his prosperity and cut off his descendants from reigning. He curses him comparing him to evil kings that God severely judged and condemned. He also condemns him from worshipping idols.

1 Kings 21: 20 And he answered, "I have found you, because you have sold
yourself to work evil in the sight of the Lord. 21 'See, I will bring disaster
upon you and will take away your posterity and will cut off all your males,
both free and slave, who are left in Israel, 22 and will make your house like
the house of Jeroboam the son of Nebat and like the house of Baasha the son of Ahijah, for the provocation with which you have provoked Me to anger and made Israel to sin.'
23 "The Lord also spoke of Jezebel, saying, 'The dogs will eat Jezebel by the wall of Jezreel.'
24 "Those from Ahab's family who die in the city will be eaten by dogs, and those who die in the field will be eaten by birds of the air."
25 But there were none compared to Ahab, who sold himself to evil deeds
in the sight of the Lord, which Jezebel his wife stirred up. 26 He performed
the most abominable act in following idols like the Amorites, whom the

Lord cast out before the children of Israel.

The Word of the prophet Elijah

God's judgements are just and true. They pierce the hardness of Ahab's heart and he fears God. As evil and wicked as he has been and is, he turns in repentance to God. He repented by tearing his clothes, a sign of repentance and death of old self. He humbles himself to God and fasted and prayed. He changed. He truly repented turning to God for mercy.

1 Kings 21: 27 When Ahab heard those words, he tore his clothes and put on sackcloth on his flesh and fasted and lay in sackcloth and walked meekly. God speaks to the prophet Elijah.

Because God saw the true repentance of an evil king, he shows mercy towards Abab and lets him live the rest of his days without the curses. The curses are still on his descendants though. Imagine if Ahab would have not only repented, but put an end to Jezabel, and had torn doen the temples to the idols. If he had wholly turned to God with all aspects of life and pleaded for a godly family, I believe God in his mercy would have acknowledged him. Through this horrible revelation of the evil king Ahab who repents and God forgives, we should know God's mercy is more than anything. God truly hears the prayers of the righteous. A person who truly repents, God will not turn away.

1 Kings 21: 28 The word of the Lord came to Elijah the Tishbite, saying, 29 "See how Ahab humbles himself before Me? Because he humbles himself before Me, I will not bring the disaster during his lifetime, but during his son's lifetime I will bring the disaster on his household."

David

Saul received David after he had slain the giant Goliath. David played the harp and sang songs that comforted Saul. The anointing of God was on David to be the next king. David knew it but Saul did not. Saul coveted David's fame and renown David became a mighty captain in Saul's army. He was an excellent warrior and was a faithful servant to God. Because David was a champion of Israel, the women loved him; the men liked him. He was a popular hero. Saul overheard the chants and songs of the common people concerning David. It angered him because he believed they were insulting him directly. He coveted the fame and popularity of David. He would have liked to be the most popular. It was a mixture of pride and covetousness.

1 Samuel 18: 6 When they came home, as David was returning from slaying the Philistine, the women came out from all cities of Israel to meet King Saul, singing and dancing, with tambourines, with joy, and with musical instruments. 7 The dancing women sang and said,
"Saul has slain his thousands,
and David his ten thousands."
8 Saul became very angry, and this saying was displeasing to him.
Therefore he said, "They have ascribed to David ten thousands, but to me they have ascribed thousands. Now what remains for him to have but the kingdom?" 9 So Saul was suspicious of David from that day and forward.

Saul began watching David with new eyes. He did not see him in the same way. He had hatred in his heart towards David and considered him a threat to his kingdom. If he believed that, he should have directly spoken to David about any aspect of loyalty or trust. He could have let David go elsewhere. He could have done many other things. What he chose to do is let the sin of covetousness and jealousy burn within him until one day an evil spirit possessed that evil heart and he threw a javelin at David trying to kill him. He gives no reason. It is covetousness that was not repented of or brought to the light. It meant the start of a horrible period in David's life, so that for many years, he had to run from Saul who was trying to kill him

.

1 Samuel 18: 10 It came to pass the following day, that an evil spirit from God came upon Saul, so that he raved in the midst of the house. And David was playing the lyre, as at other times. Now there was a spear in Saul's hand. 11 And Saul threw the spear. For he said, "I will pin David to the wall." But David avoided him two times.

Absalom coveted David's throne

After Absalom returned to Israel but David did not let him come into his place in the palace, Absalom became covetousness of David's throne. He began a conspiracy of trying to win the hearts of the people of Israel by agreeing with their complaints and pointing to himself as a solution. He was doing treason against his own family. He was collecting an army of people who agreed with him.

2 Samuel 15: 1 After this Absalom acquired for himself a chariot, horses, and fifty men to run before him. 2 Absalom would go early and stand beside the way into the gate. When any man who had a dispute concerning which he had come to the king for a judgment approached, Absalom would call to him and say, "Which city are you from?" And he would say, "Your servant is from one of the tribes of Israel." 3 Then Absalom would say to

him, "Look, your claim is good and right, but there is no one to hear you on behalf of the king." 4 Absalom would continue, "If I were appointed a judge in the land, then every man who had a claim could come and I would give him justice."
5 When a man would approach to bow before him, he would reach out, embrace him, and kiss him. 6 Absalom acted this way toward every Israelite who came to the king for a judgment. So Absalom stole the hearts of the men of Israel.

Absalom committed the sin for 40 years until he had gathered a large army. He planned an attack on the palace to overthrow the King. His covetousness was turned into treachery against his own family. His attack on David (anointed King placed there by God) results in his own violent death.

2 Samuel 15: 10 But Absalom sent scouts throughout all of the tribes of Israel, saying, "When you hear the sound of the horn, say: Absalom has become king in Hebron." 11 Now two hundred men went with Absalom from Jerusalem, invited and unsuspecting; they did not know anything. 12 Absalom sent for Ahithophel the Gilonite, the advisor of David, from his city Giloh, while he was offering the sacrifices. Now the conspiracy was strong, for the number of people with Absalom was continually growing.

David coveted Uriah's wife

King David could have had any woman he wanted. There would be many women who would desire to be intimate with the king. He desired the wife of Uriah. He didn't just want a beautiful woman; he lusted after Uriah's wife. He got her to come lie with him while her husband was away fighting for Israel. Because of the first sin of desiring another man's wife, he ends up signing a letter to kill Uriah because he does not want to repent for desiring Bathsheba and Bathsheba is with child, while her husband had no relations with her. It is a way of protecting Bathsheba from certain death; it is a way to avoid repentance; he is the king; he abuses his authority.

2 Samuel 11: 2 One evening when David arose from his bed and was walking on the roof of the king's house, from the roof he saw a woman bathing; and the woman was very beautiful. 3 So, David sent someone to inquire about the woman. And it was asked, "Is this not Bathsheba the daughter of Eliam, the wife of Uriah the Hittite?" 4 So David sent messengers, and took her; and she came to him, and he lay with her. When she had purified herself from her uncleanness, she returned to her house. 5 The woman conceived. So she sent a message and reported to David, "I am

pregnant."

The result of this sin of covetousness, adultery and murder is that David is judged severely by God. He received strife into his family because of his deeds.

Pharisees coveted Jesus popularity with the people

The Pharisees were jealous of Jesus and their covetousness for his popularity became evident in their attempts to trap him with words and on several occasions, they tried to kill him but he passed through the midst of them. Even though some of them witnessed the miracles and healing of Jesus, they did not believe in him. Rather than learn from Jesus' teaching, they tried to trick him by getting him to sin against God's word. Even after they were eye witnesses to Jesus raising Lazarus (who had been dead for 3 days) from the dead, they did not believe Jesus was the Messiah. They hated him because he was popular with the people and he was teaching the people about God although he had not attended religious schooling.

Directly after Jesus had raised Lazarus from the tomb the reaction of some was negative. Rather than desire to know him or how he was doing the miracles, rather than praying, they conspired to kill Jesus.

John 11: 46 But some of them went away to the Pharisees and told them
what Jesus had done. 47 Then the chief priests and the Pharisees assembled
the Sanhedrin and said, "What shall we do? This Man is performing many
signs. 48 If we leave Him alone like this, everyone will believe in Him, and
the Romans will come and take away both our temple and our nation."
49 Then one of them named Caiaphas, who was the high priest that year,
said to them, "You know nothing at all, 50 nor do you consider that it is
expedient for us that one man should die for the people, that the whole
nation should not perish."
51 He did not say this on his own authority. But being the high priest that
year, he prophesied that Jesus would die for the nation, 52 and not for the
nation only, but that He might also gather together in unity the children of
God who were scattered abroad. 53 So from that day forward they planned
to put Him to death.
John 12: 17 Now the crowd that was with Him when He called Lazarus out
of the tomb and raised him from the dead bore witness. 18 The crowd went
and met Him for this reason: They heard that He had performed this sign.
19 So the Pharisees said among themselves, "See, you are gaining nothing!
Look, the world has followed Him!"

Peter warns against false prophets

The apostle Peter could recognize false prophets because he knew Jesus. God gave him warning to give to the church that there would be false prophets and teachers who would use the people for selfish gain. They would exploit the people because of greed or covetousness. He warns the people giving the fruit of such false prophets.

2 Peter 2: 2 But there were also false prophets among the people, just as there will be false teachers among you, who will secretly bring in destructive heresies, even denying the Lord who bought them, bringing swift destruction upon themselves. 2 And many will follow their destructive ways, because of whom the way of truth will be blasphemed. 3 And in their greed they will exploit you with deceptive words. Their judgment, made long ago, does not linger, and their destruction does not slumber.

Covetousness

Covetousness is a sin that leads to other sins, unless the person repents. As soon as you see something beautiful that you desire, ask God to bless you with one just like it. God is merciful and would be glad to give it to you. It's a way of not coveting.

Conclusion

It is my prayer that my book has given you insight into scriptural understanding of the Commandments and how important they are to a godly life. Through the Holy Spirit living on the inside of us, God is able to allow us to live holy. It is only by living in the Spirit of God with the plumb line of God's word that we are able to live without sin. Jesus made the way so that we could be free from sin and all the consequences of it.

PRAYERS

The following prayers are samples of prayers you could pray for important reasons. You could pray the same meaning in your own words. The prayers are meant as examples only.

PRAYER FOR SALVATION

Thank you- Jesus that you died for me on the cross. Thank you that you rose from the dead and ascended into heaven. Thank you that you are coming back again. I thank you Jesus for forgiving my sins. Thank you for your blood that cleanses me from all sin and unrighteousness. Thank you that your blood makes me holy. Thank you for saving me. Fill me with the Holy Spirit to overflowing. I pray for the baptism of the Holy Spirit. Lead me to other people who love you and serve you and that can help me know more about you. Give me the discerning of spirits strong. I thank you and praise you. With my mouth, I confess Jesus Christ is my LORD. Amen.

PRAYER FOR BAPTISM OF THE HOLY SPIRIT

Thank you- Jesus that you promised to send the gift of the Holy Spirit to us. Thank you that this promise is to all believers. I am a believer. I want all of you that you will give me. I want to know you God. Baptize me in the Holy Spirit with the evidence of speaking in other tongues. I believe you want to fill me to overflowing with your Spirit so that I might be an effective witness for Christ on the earth. Thank you for saving me. Thank you for your Holy presence. [begin praising God for what He has done for you – sing worship choruses and praise God in your natural language. Believe that He is present with you – start praising and worshipping Him. As phrases come to you in other tongues, say them – praise God with new tongues.] I praise you. I thank you. I receive the baptism of the Holy Spirit.

PRAYER FOR RELEASING ANGELS

God, I thank you that angels are ministering spirits sent as ministers to us. I pray over my prayer request NAME IT HERE. God I pray release angels to perform it. I thank you for releasing the answer to me. I praise you for it. Amen.

PRAYER FOR RESISTING EVIL

I am the redeemed of the LORD. Jesus Christ has saved me. I am a new creation in Christ Jesus. Jesus blood covers me. I live in the spirit. The Holy Spirit of God fills my spirit. O Holy Spirit quicken me; give me wisdom. Pray [expecting God will give you discerning of spirits so you will have the right words to speak.]

In the name of Jesus Christ, I bind you. I rebuke you evil spirit. In the name of Jesus, I command you to go out. You have no place in my life. I cast you out. You have no place with me. I am covered by the blood of Jesus and His righteousness is my righteousness. Go out evil spirit in the name of Jesus Christ!

Thank you, Holy spirit for your holy presence. Release angels to drive out the enemy. Thank you. Amen.

PRAYER FOR PROTECTION

Holy Spirit release angels to protect me. I plead the blood of Jesus over me. I pray the protection you promise to your people. Cover me Jesus. Holy Spirit give me wisdom, discernment and understanding. Thank you for angels that guard over me. Thank you for your blood that protects me and a hedge of protection around me. I praise you O God. [praise God with some worship choruses and expect God's holy presence to be manifest in you]. Thank you. O God for protection.

PRAYER FOR HEALING

Lord Jesus, Thank you that you gave your life for me so that I can be saved, healed and delivered. I thank your for the scripture that by your stripes I am healed. I thank you for my healing.

NAME THE DISEASE I bind you in the name of Jesus. I cast you out. I pray over myself that I would be whole spirit, soul and body.

Thank you God for your healing manifestation in my life. I give you all the glory. Amen.

PRAYER OF REPENTENCE

Jesus, thank you for your blood shed for me. I repent of the sin of NAME IT. I thank you for liberty from sin. I cut off the root of iniquity in my family. I thank you for your empowering presence to live a Holy life. Holy Spirit lead and guide me in the paths of righteousness. Thank you for giving me godly desires. Let my life align with your word. In Jesus name. Amen.

OTHER BOOKS BY CHRIS LEGEBOW

Available on Amazon.ca Amazon.com or Amazon.ca or Kindle
Or the Create Space webstore.

Living Word Publishers

Angels: Ministering Spirits

An Excellent Spirit: Living Life Wholly Unto God

Covenant With God: God's Relationship With Man

Discovering and Using your Spiritual Gifts

Divine Healing in the Scriptures: God's Mercy Towards Man

The Commandments

The Doctrine of Christ: Essential Truths of Scripture

The Five-Fold Ministry: Gifts to the Church

Kinds of Prayer. Knowing Them and Using Them Effectively

Living Life Fully: Knowing your Purpose

The Anointing: the Glory of God

The High Calling: Life Worth Living

The Sacraments: A Charismatic Guide

ABOUT THE AUTHOR

Chris Legebow is a Christian Professor of English and Communications. She has taught at the elementary, high school and College and University levels. She has ministered in her local churches in intercessory prayer, teaching Sunday school and other Christian Doctrine classes to children and youths. She has preached to congregations and given her testimony. Although she was not raised in a Christian home, she came to know Jesus Christ as her Saviour and LORD while she was studying in University. This radically transformed her life in terms of priorities and commitment. She has a strong passion for the great commission – that Jesus Christ would be preached throughout all the earth believing that it a major sign of the LORD's return. She has been a part of several different types of full gospel charismatic churches but has also gained much of her insight and enlightenment from Christian Media and broadcasting. She hopes to continue ministering, serving, interceding and giving and teaching until the LORD returns.

www.ingramcontent.com/pod-product-compliance
Lightning Source LLC
Chambersburg PA
CBHW021206020426
42331CB00003B/232
9781988914039